THE

W9-DEW-029

A
GUIDE
TO
ESSAYS
AND
PAPERS

THE

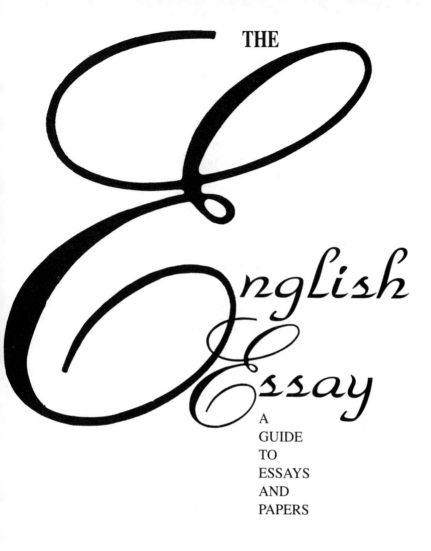

English
Essay

A
GUIDE
TO
ESSAYS
AND
PAPERS

Hugh Robertson

McGraw-Hill Ryerson Limited

Toronto Montreal New York Auckland Bogotá
Caracas Lisbon London Madrid Mexico Milan New Delhi
Paris San Juan Singapore Sydney Tokyo

THE ENGLISH ESSAY
A Guide to Essays and Papers

ISBN 0-07-551417-6

1 2 3 4 5 6 7 8 9 0 D 2 1 0 9 8 7 6 5 4 3

Printed and bound in Canada

Care has been taken to trace ownership of copyright material contained in this text. The publishers will gladly accept any information that will enable them to rectify any reference or credit in subsequent editions.

Canadian Cataloguing in Publication Data
Robertson, Hugh, date—
    The English essay: a guide to essays and papers

Includes bibliographical references.
ISBN 0-07-551417-6

1. Report writing. 2. Exposition (Rhetoric).
I. Title.

LB2369.R63 1992   808'.02   C92-094777-8

PUBLISHER: JANICE MATTHEWS
ASSOCIATE EDITOR: NANCY CHRISTOFFER
SENIOR SUPERVISING EDITOR: CAROL ALTILIA
COPY EDITOR: EDIE FRANKS
COVER AND INTERIOR DESIGN: MATTHEWS COMMUNICATIONS DESIGN

This book was manufactured in Canada using acid-free and recycled paper.

Printed and bound in Canada by
John Deyell Company Limited.

*To my wife and sons
for their unending
support and patience.*

ACKNOWLEDGEMENTS

A number of people kindly perused the manuscript of *The English Essay*. I am indebted to the following persons for their instructive comments and suggestions: Pamela Bentley, Danielle Bertrand, Neil Graham, Tony Horava, Wayne Howell, Bruce Lynch, Professor Karen McFadden and her students, Peter Peart, Hugh Penton, Joanne Peters, Peter Sheppard, Peter Smith, Suzanne St-Jacques, Jon Terpening, and Patricia Williams.

I am especially grateful to Professor Karen McFadden for her perceptive comments and invaluable advice. I would also like to express my sincere thanks to Dr. Wayne Howell for his kind assistance in the preparation of the manuscript; his expertise, erudition, and good humour were much appreciated.

I would like to add a special word of thanks to Janice Matthews and Nancy Christoffer of McGraw-Hill Ryerson for their assistance throughout the project.

CONTENTS

INTRODUCTION

From secondary school to graduate school, essay writing is a central part of English courses. Writing successful essays is not an easy task. However, there are procedures to make it less difficult and transform it into a stimulating learning experience.

The English Essay takes you step by step through the entire process of writing a formal essay or term paper. Using a single example, you will be guided through launching the essay, locating sources, gathering ideas and information, organizing the material, and composing a thesis or argument. The example is an essay on the work of Alice Munro, a Canadian short story writer whose work has gained international acclaim. This manual emphasizes that an essay is an argument, not a descriptive narrative, an anthology of quotations, or a simple presentation of facts.

The process described in this book is the result of many years of teaching students of various ages. It has been tried and tested. An English literature topic is used to demonstrate the approach, but the method can be used for most essays and term papers in other academic disciplines. Although this manual emphasizes the importance of having an argument or thesis, the method can be modified for descriptive and narrative assignments, reports, reviews, examinations, and seminars.

Writing an essay gives you an opportunity to explore ideas and exercise critical judgement. In the process you will develop valuable skills: the ability to locate, organize, and communicate information, and the ability to argue successfully. These skills are useful not only in school, they are life-skills of great relevance and wide application.

While *The English Essay* outlines a process by which you can confidently tackle most assignments and provides advice on quotations, citations, style, and format, it is not exhaustive. You may wish to consult the latest editions of one or more of the following manuals for more detailed information on certain aspects of the writing process. There is a more extensive list of recommended resources in Style, section VI.

> *MLA Handbook for Writers of Research Papers* by Joseph Gibaldi and Walter S. Achtert.
>
> *A Manual for Writers of Term Papers, Theses, and Dissertations* by Kate L. Turabian.
>
> *McGraw-Hill Handbook of English* by Harry Shaw.

Tell me, I will forget
Show me, I may remember
Involve me, I will understand

Chinese proverb

PREPARING THE ESSAY

INTRODUCTION

There is no shortage of types of writing assignments in English courses nor is there a shortage of terms used by teachers to describe the various types of assignments. The terminology can be confusing. For instance, does an assignment to write an "expository essay" mean that you are to relate information on a subject with which you are familiar; does it mean you are to state a point of view based mainly on your own experience; or does it mean you are to argue a point of view, citing various authors as you do so? What is an "analytical essay," a "critical essay," an "interpretive essay"?

Unfortunately, there is no consensus—even among English instructors—as to the precise meaning of these terms. Thus, it is imperative that you determine exactly what is expected from you before beginning an assignment. Find out from your instructor if you are expected to do research and, if so, is the research to be confined to primary source materials (literary texts) or are you expected to consult secondary sources, such as other books, journals, and audio-visual materials?

This manual assumes that your assignment is either to focus solely on a primary text or to conduct some research involving that text. The purpose of the assignment is to produce an essay that develops and sustains a point of view, thesis, or argument.

The type of research required will depend on the type of essay you choose or are assigned. Not only are literary works subject to a variety of approaches and interpretations, they can be analyzed and appreciated on moral, philosophical, and political grounds, to name just a few. Hence it is quite possible that your research will take you into many different areas.

On the other hand, it is possible that your investigation may be confined solely to a single text. Your instructor may ask that you subjectively interpret an assigned poem, short story, play, or novel without consulting other sources. In this instance, your instructor is inviting a fresh interpretation of the text—one arising out of your own personality and life experiences not crafted from the thoughts and critical judgements of others. If you are given an essay assign-ment of this type, your attention will be directed exclusively to the assigned primary text. Nevertheless, you will find the methods described in this manual useful, for you will still be required to record and organize ideas and information relevant to your thesis or argument.

No matter what the nature of the assignment, you must not fail to give the primary text the attention it deserves. Do not give it a quick read and then run off to the library to see what other persons have said about it. Your careful reading of the text might have resulted in a genuinely fresh insight. Although a particular literary text—Shakespeare's *Hamlet*, for instance—has been stud-ied by scholars and students for centuries, still you can find something original to say about it.

Art scholars have been studying Michelangelo's Sistine Chapel paintings for over four hundred years, but it was only a few years ago that a tourist pointed out something that had eluded everyone else: in the "Creation of Adam" scene—the famous one in which God extends his arm and gives the spark of life to Adam's outreached finger—the composition of the figures around the Deity represents, with quite remarkable accuracy, the shape of the human brain. If you look carefully at a literary text through the prism of your own life and experience, you might be surprised at what you can discover.

There is no "last word" on any literary text: all readers who bring their emotions and intellects to bear on a work of literary art are capable of providing unique insights. But if you wish to communicate your insights to others so that they can understand and appreciate them, you must develop a system for recording and organizing ideas. Furthermore, you must develop the writing skills to convey your interpretations to the reader in a clear and logical manner.

SELECTING THE TOPIC

Your instructor may assign the topic for an essay or may permit selection from a list of topics. Sometimes students may choose their own topics. If you are allowed to select a topic, choose one that holds some interest for you and offers you a challenge.

If the topic has been assigned by your instructor, certain constraints may be imposed on you. The assignment may be general or very specific. It may be in the form of a title, proposition, provocative statement, question, or quotation. **Decode carefully any key words such as "analyze," "evaluate," or "discuss" in an assigned topic.**

Once you have decided on the topic for your essay, clarify it with your instructor. At the same time, discuss the following:

- The exact nature of the assignment including whether secondary sources are required.

- The meaning of any ambiguous terms such as "analyze," "discuss," "interpret," and "evaluate."

- The citation or documentation procedures required.

- The length of the completed paper.

- The due date and whether extensions are permitted.

- The overall structure, such as the nature of the introduction and whether a concluding summary is necessary.

- The criteria for assessment and whether a sample evaluation form is available.

- Any other relevant matters, such as the use of the first person.

- Specific manuscript requirements, such as a typed final copy as opposed to a handwritten one.

Regular contact with your instructor should be maintained until the paper is completed. Since requirements will vary among instructors, you might consider making a copy of the above list and checking off the various items during discussions with your instructor.

As soon as the due date is established, start planning a schedule for the completion of the various stages of the paper. Advance planning is critical, since you are unlikely to learn much or derive any satisfaction if your essay is written in frenzied haste the night before the assignment is due.

DEFINING THE FOCUS

If your instructor has not provided you with a specific issue, your first task is to narrow down the topic. Focus on one significant aspect—an important problem or a major interpretation. It may be that your reading of the primary text—or texts—has already provided you with a focus. However, if you know very little about your topic, it will be necessary to do some preliminary reading to isolate an issue for investigation. Along with the primary text, surveys of literature and encyclopedias are useful for this exploratory reading.[1] In addition, you might consult library indexes which are explained in the next section.

The entries under your topic heading in these indexes will provide you with many interesting leads. Also, you can assemble a group of fellow students to brainstorm essay issues and bounce around ideas. It is a useful practice to keep a log, writing folder, or an Ideas and Questions Notebook—an "I.Q. Journal"—in which to jot down ideas.

Narrowing is a vital stage in the process because the issue you select will provide the focus for your investigation. It is important to devote your attention to a manageable aspect that is not too big and not too small. You should also avoid issues that lend themselves to a largely narrative, descriptive, or biographical approach. Controversial issues can work well because they are usually widely written about, and they provide an opportunity to test conflicting interpretations, perspectives, and values. It is also a good idea to have one or two backup issues in case you run into difficulties with your first choice.

Frequently, this narrowing or focusing process will involve more than one stage. For example, your reading of Munro's short stories might lead you to identify certain recurrent themes in her fiction, but an essay exploring those themes in all of her stories would not be an essay, it would be a book. It is unlikely that you would have the time to do the necessary reading for such a project, let alone to write the essay. That is why it is essential that you narrow the focus. Start by exploring the topic through the field of wide-angle binoculars, but move toward studying your issue through the narrow focus of a telescope. You could consider, for instance, the possibility of exploring the recurrent themes in just one of Munro's short stories.

Narrowing the focus is crucial, even if your essay deals with only a single primary text.

POSING A QUESTION

Once you have narrowed your topic and identified an important issue, you should begin your investigation by posing an incisive and probing question based on your topic. If your topic has been assigned by the instructor, consider rephrasing it in question form.

The formulation of the question is crucial to the development of the essay, because it is the nature of the question that defines the scope and focus of the essay. The nature of the question also influences the length of the essay, and this is something you should also bear in mind: if you are expected to produce a short paper, do not pose a question that can be answered only at length.

The question must be clear, precise, and free of ambiguities. If it has these qualities it will give direction and purpose to the assignment and guide you in your search for a convincing answer to the question you have posed. **The answer to your question will form your thesis.**

Avoid questions that lead to straight narration, description, or biography such as "How does romantic poetry differ from epic poetry?" or "Who was Flannery O'Connor?" Also, do not choose questions of a speculative nature such as "Would Alice Munro's stories be different if she had grown up in the American south?" because there can be no conclusive or credible answers to conjectures of this nature.

Take care to avoid questions that may be based on unfounded assumptions such as "Why does Ernest Hemingway fail as a novelist?" The assumption here is that the novels are failures rather than successes. That might be a difficult point to argue effectively since it is contrary to the view of most people who have considered the issue, including the Nobel Prize Committee. This is not to say that you should not argue it; you have a right to your opinions. However, you should bear in mind that you have set yourself a difficult task. In this particular instance, a task much less daunting and far more promising would be to pose the question "Why is *Across The River and Into The Trees* Hemingway's weakest novel?"

Always try to pose a single challenging question that demands analysis and argument—a question that can be stated briefly and succinctly in just one sentence. Avoid compound or multiple questions.

If you have difficulty in shaping a good question, it may be necessary to do additional reading. Further brainstorming sessions with fellow students can help to expand your range of options. Maintain a list of potential questions in your I.Q. Journal (Ideas and Questions Notebook). Finally, after having chosen your question, check again with your instructor to ensure that it is acceptable and appropriately phrased.

Let us return to our example, the short stories of Alice Munro. Assuming that our interest is in her critical and popular success, we might formulate the question as follows: Why are Alice Munro's short stories about rural Ontario of interest to an international readership?

The direction is now set. Your task is to develop an answer to the question. Your answer will take the form of a "thesis" or "argument."

Some manuals suggest starting the process of preparing an essay by proposing a thesis. The difficulty with this approach is that you must have the background knowledge to suggest a sound thesis as a starting point. Furthermore, there is the temptation to select material to support your position, while rejecting material that runs counter to it.*

Launching your project with a precise question such as "Why are Alice Munro's short stories about rural Ontario of interest to an international readership?" opens up a wider range of possibilities than starting from a fixed position such as "Alice Munro's fictional technique is responsible for her broad readership." It might be useful to remember Sherlock Holmes' advice: never theorize in advance of the facts.

---

*Certain types of assignments do lend themselves to launching the process with a thesis or proposition. However, avoid starting with an "educated guess" and then selecting information "to prove the thesis." It is intellectual dishonesty to consciously select material that supports a preselected position and reject information that runs counter to it.

LOCATING SOURCES

Once the central question has been established, the next step is to start compiling a list of potential sources of information. Primary sources usually present no problem, since major literary works are widely available. However, if your question requires that you consult an early or minor work by a writer—a work that may be long out of print—it pays to determine whether you can obtain a copy before committing yourself to that particular question.

If your assignment requires that you deal with a single primary text only, then you need not be concerned about consulting other sources. You should proceed to the Preparatory Reading section on page 18.

If your assignment requires that you consult secondary sources, there may be a question as to how many would be appropriate. Your instructor may have imposed a minimum or maximum number. If not, you should judge by the scope of your question how many sources are necessary. It is important to determine as soon as possible whether sufficient sources are available for you to deal with the question you have posed.

Libraries can appear overwhelming, but there is no need to panic. If introductory tours are available, start by signing up for a tour of your library and then later wander around on your own, familiarizing yourself with the layout. Many libraries provide handouts on everything from regulations to lists of reference materials. Develop a collection of these information sheets and read them carefully. Approach the library staff if you have difficulties. They are specialists with the expertise to answer your questions. Their advice and suggestions will save hours of your time.

The catalogue is the main source of bibliographic information in libraries. It is usually the best place to start your search. Catalogues are either based on the Library of Congress system or on the Dewey Decimal system. Increasingly, libraries are replacing their card catalogues with databases of computer-readable records accessible through terminals. On-line computer catalogues offer greater versatility for searching than the traditional author/title and subject divisions of the card system.

Skilful use of an on-line catalogue will turn up a wide variety of material in the library—books, periodicals, and bibliographies. Some libraries also have a backup microfiche catalogue* for use when the computers are down.

Although on-line searching provides increased accessibility to material in the library, it is only one of the tools available to you as a researcher. Most libraries carry a variety of bibliographic aids ranging from periodical and newspaper indexes to data base searching and registers of translations. To avoid diverting you from the research process by describing these aids in detail here, they have been placed in the Appendix. Read pages 103 to 111 carefully. Familiarize yourself with all the available bibliographic tools and research resources.

Do not be overwhelmed by the range of bibliographic aids described in the Appendix. You are likely to use only a few of these initially. As you do essay assignments during your high school and undergraduate years, try to get exposure to as many of these resources as possible. Test them out in your library: hands-on practical experience is a far better teacher than a manual.

As you work through the bibliographic aids you will be searching for sources pertinent to your question. Knowing which bibliographic aids exist in your research field will not only save time but will allow you to build a wide-ranging list of sources. And, of course, a knowledge of the various bibliographic aids will make it easier for you to write subsequent essays.

There are two recommended methods of building the working bibliography: you can use standard notepaper or you can use index cards. The bibliographic information can be listed in exactly the same way on both notepaper and index cards. Choose the method that best suits your needs. There is an alternative method using a computer and a modem that is explained on page 16.

---

*"Catalogue" is used in this manual to refer to all three systems: card, on-line, and microfiche.

INDEX CARD METHOD

As you discover potential sources of information in your searching, list them on separate cards and fill in all the essential bibliographic details as follows:

- Continue listing all your sources on separate cards in this manner.

- The Codes AM and IKB represent key words in the titles and they are used to identify the sources.

- Enter the library and catalogue number once the source is located.

- Check off the source once it has been used.

NOTEPAPER METHOD

As you discover potential sources of information in your searching, list them on standard notepaper and fill in all the essential bibliographic details as follows:

CODE	Working Bibliography
POL	Munro, Alice. *The Progress of Love.* Toronto: McClelland and Stewart, 1986 Public Library PS8775.U57P76
AM	Blodgett, E.D. *Alice Munro.* Boston: Twayne, 1988. School Library PS852.U46Z58 ✓
UIM	Hoy,Helen. "Alice Munro: Unforgettable Indigestible Messages." *Journal of Canadian Studies* 26.1 (1991): 5-21. Community College Library
IKB	Interview with Kay Bonetti. American Audio Prose Library Inc. Columbia, MO, June 1987. University Audio Visual Library 89-A-00023 CASAM

- Continue listing all your sources in this manner.

- The Codes represent key words in the titles and they are used to identify the sources.

- Enter the library and catalogue number once the source is located.

- Check off the source once it has been used.

Index cards are more versatile than notepaper. It is easier to compile the final Bibliography or Works Cited from separate cards rather than from notepaper. Once the source has been used, one can indicate on the reverse side of the card whether it is primary or secondary material and comment critically on the value of the source to the research.

To expand the range and diversity of your sources you can classify them in groups such as books, periodicals, general (neither book nor periodical, such as a university thesis), non-print or primary. You can then use different coloured index cards: for example, blue for books and yellow for periodicals, to identify the different categories of sources.

If you are using notepaper for your working bibliography, you can classify your sources in a similar way by devoting a separate page to each category. Simply head your pages Books, Periodicals, and so forth, and write in the source details as shown on page 15.

Instead of notepaper and index cards, you can use a computer and a modem. Modems allow you to search library holdings and other databases directly from your computer through a telephone link. If you have conducted your searches by means of a modem, and have obtained print-outs, you should transfer the print-outs to cards or notepaper either by writing them out or by cutting and pasting them up in different categories as explained above. Alternatively, you can route the sources to disk instead of printing them. Then you can create separate files for the different categories such as books and periodicals and transfer the sources to the respective files.

Do not attempt to place your sources in alphabetical order at this stage; merely list them as you discover them. Enter all the publication details for each source accurately because these details will be required for the final bibliography. If you do this conscientiously, there will be no need to relocate the sources to check the details, and waste valuable time.

There is also no need at this stage to write up the bibliographic details in their final format. However, if you wish to save time later, read pages 61–87 and decide which citation or documentation system to use. Frequently, your instructor will indicate the system you are expected to use.

Combine tradition, technology, and tenacity in combing the various bibliographic aids for sources. Judicious use of these aids will save you hours of frustrating searching and you will be surprised at the quantity of information you can assemble on almost any topic.

When searching for sources consider books and periodicals, print and nonprint sources, primary and secondary information, old and new material. The range of your sources can enhance the quality of your essay dramatically. You will undoubtedly experience obstacles and frustrations in digging for material, but do not give up: the tenacious researcher is invariably rewarded.

At this stage you are simply listing the titles and details of potential sources of information on one of notepaper, index cards, or computer. As yet there is no need to find the material unless you fear someone else is going to clean out the library holdings on your topic. Once you have assured yourself that there are adequate sources available, you are ready to move on to the next phase. However, if there are insufficient sources, you will have to change your question and probably the issue as well. You can appreciate the advantage in having a backup issue and question in reserve. It is very frustrating to discover, a month after starting, that there are insufficient sources to build a paper. By determining the extent of potential sources at this early stage you will not be subjected to the agony of exhausting your sources halfway through your research and then having to start anew with the deadline looming even closer.

Compilation of the working bibliography does not stop at this stage—it is an ongoing process. You will probably keep adding useful sources to your list throughout the research.

PREPARATORY READING

You should thoroughly acquaint yourself with the literary text that is the subject of your analysis before reading widely in secondary sources. Focus on what the author wrote and on what the words mean to you, not on what others have said about the author's writing.

There is no right or wrong way to react to a literary text. All readers bring their own emotional and intellectual background to their encounters with a text, and there is no telling in advance what sparks—if any—will fly as a result of the encounters. But you have to give the text a chance. Literature is capable of stimulating a reader both intellectually and emotionally. However, this stimulation is unlikely to occur if the art object is treated in a cursory manner. A person in a line of tourists herded past the Mona Lisa is unlikely to be in a position to comment on the virtues of Leonardo da Vinci's painting. Likewise, speed-reading or skip-reading a novel is unlikely to result in any useful insight or emotional response. A careful initial reading can often result in a genuinely fresh insight or feeling.

If the object of your study is a poem, then you should read it several times. Read the poem aloud; try to hear the poet's voice. Read with a dictionary at hand. Make sure you know what every word means or, in the case of a poem written many years ago, what every word meant at the time it was written. Enter your comments and responses in your I.Q. Journal.

If the object of your study is a short story, read it as carefully as you would read a poem. Bear in mind that a short story is not a mininovel; a short story has its own structure and form. A study of its structure can often lead to interesting insights. Unless your instructor has asked you specifically to concentrate on the one story only, you should read some other short stories by the same author. Often, the reading of other stories will trigger insights about the story that is the subject of your essay.

If the object of your study is a novel or a literary work of novel-length proportions, then make sure you read the entire text at least once. Read with pen in hand, jotting down your own thoughts, questions, or responses in your I.Q. Journal or recording them in some other manner. If you own the book and if you don't mind marking it, make notes right in the margins. If you don't want to mark the book, consider buying a supply of self-stick removable notes and using them to mark particular pages. **It is important that you conscientiously record your initial responses to the text in some manner.**

While you are engaged in the preparatory reading, keep the question or purpose of the assignment uppermost in your mind. Be guided by the purpose as you jot down your reactions and responses. A central argument or thesis may begin to emerge: get it down no matter how shadowy or indistinct it might be. Likewise, a tentative structure for the essay might start to appear: sketch it out in your I.Q. Journal.

For instance, preparatory reading for the Munro essay involved the reading of several of her short stories. During this reading it was noted that the stories quite often dealt with the unveiling of hidden truths about how society really worked. Tentatively, these "unveilings" were grouped into three categories, having to do with family, community, and religion. The preparatory reading also showed the essay could possibly be structured on an analysis of a single short story, "The Progress of Love," since that one story dealt with unveilings in all three of the tentatively identified categories.

Your preparatory reading could include reference works such as encyclopedias, biographical dictionaries, and general surveys of literature. Reading about your issue and about the author in these works will provide you with background knowledge you can use to develop perceptive questions. It also will provide you with a basis for judging what is relevant and important in the answers.

You are not doing formal research at this stage; you are doing this reading to acquaint yourself with the issue, the text, and the author. And, most important, you are gauging your emotional and intellectual responses. These initial responses, which may be powerfully felt but dimly understood, will become more clearly perceived as you subject the text to critical analysis.

Also, you might discover another aspect of your topic that is more interesting and challenging than your original choice. If the alternative issue is more compelling than the original, do not hesitate to change direction by shifting the focus and formulating another question.

RECORDING INFORMATION AND IDEAS

Armed with a thorough understanding of your subject from your preparatory reading, an incisive question, and a substantial working bibliography (if you are doing an assignment that requires secondary sources), you are now ready to start analyzing* your material and recording your responses. The preliminary work is necessary: there are no short cuts.

Since you cannot remember everything you read, a systematic method of recording ideas and information is essential. This is true whether you are focusing on only a primary text or using secondary sources. It is impossible to develop a good essay without an organized collection of notes.

As you work your way through the analytical phase, bear in mind that your sole task is to develop a thoughtful and convincing answer to the central question. The answer will form your thesis. Record only information and ideas that appear relevant to the question. However, guard against prejudice: if you consciously select information that supports only one particular point of view, you will not produce a balanced essay.

If you are using secondary sources, you must track down the sources listed in your working bibliography. The major sources such as books and periodicals can be located through the main catalogue, but others such as taped interviews might require the assistance of a librarian. Do not worry if you cannot find all your sources, as it is unlikely they will all be available in the libraries in your community. However, if you have an extensive and wide-ranging bibliography, you should locate sufficient secondary sources to prepare your essay.

Most books can be borrowed from libraries, but other sources such as reference material, periodicals, and microfilmed newspapers have to be used in the library. As you find a source, note the

---

* Analysis is a careful scrutiny of the textual material, the isolation of relevant detail, and the identification of key ideas.

library and catalogue number in the working bibliography so that you can easily find it again if necessary.

Recorded notes are largely of three types: summaries of ideas and information, direct quotations, and personal ideas and responses. Itemized below are some suggestions to assist you in compiling your research notes.

• Add your own ideas and questions; do not just paraphrase what you read.

• Be concise, clear, and accurate.

• If you develop your own shorthand system for notemaking, ensure that your abbreviations and symbols will make sense to you later on.

• Summarize ideas and information in your own words if you are using secondary sources.

• Restrict the number of direct quotations if you are not dealing exclusively with a primary literary text.

• Transcribe direct quotations accurately.

• Indicate whether a piece of information is established fact or subjective opinion.

• Material may be interesting and it may be true but ask yourself if it is relevant to your question or purpose.

Students do not always have the time or expertise to engage in detailed and complex criticism of sources. The problem of authenticity and credibility of sources does not arise—or only rarely arises—with primary texts. However, it does arise with secondary source material. For example, how well-known is the author, or how reputable is the publishing company? Is the article published in a respected journal? Does the author treat the subject fairly? If questions such as these arise, you can ask advice from your instructor or librarian. You can also consult a review of a book to ascertain its reliability. Questions of this type will help you determine the quality of your sources.[2]

Research for English essays is not a mechanical gathering of "facts." It is a complex process requiring insight, thought, and creative imagination. You have to dissect the material and evaluate interpretations and judgements as you search for an answer to your question. Read critically: do not accept ideas and interpretations blindly. Be sceptical: read between the lines and beyond the print; question carefully the arguments and opinions of the authors. **Raise your own stimulating and challenging questions; they can yield surprising new insights.**

There are three ways that you can record information and ideas. You can use index cards, standard notepaper, or a computer. No matter which method you use, the notemaking techniques which are described in detail under "Index Cards" remain basically the same. Therefore, you should read the Index Card section carefully, even if you are using notepaper or a computer, since the notemaking techniques are not repeated in those sections.

This guide recommends the use of index cards for recording ideas and information because they are versatile, efficient, and inexpensive. The notepaper method is similar in principle to the index card method. This procedure is described on page 29. The computer method is described on page 30.

Index Card Method

You have a choice of three common sizes of index cards for your research. The smallest is most commonly used.

In the following section, the examples of notemaking on index cards are all taken from the Munro essay. As you will recall, the question had to do with the nature of the broad appeal of her short stories. The preparatory reading had suggested the appeal arose because of the way in which she dealt with the uncovering of certain social truths about family, community, and religion. Furthermore, the preparatory reading had suggested the essay could profitably focus on one short story, "The Progress of Love,"* although references would be made to other stories.

---

*Titles of books are italicized or underlined. Titles of stories in books are placed in quotation marks. In this case the reference is to the short story, "The Progress of Love," which appears in the collection of short stories entitled, *The Progress of Love*.

When you are making notes from primary source material, always use direct quotations. Do not paraphrase, since you will need to quote primary source material verbatim when you draft the essay. The reader of your essay wants to see what the author actually wrote and then your interpretation of it. The reader does not want to see your interpretation of your interpretation of what the author wrote. Transcribing the quotation accurately on the index cards means that you do not have to look it up again later in the primary source. This could prove inconvenient if it is in the library at the time you are drafting your essay.

The following example is taken from "The Progress of Love":

POL 3

"My father was so polite, even in the family. He took time to ask me how I was. Country manners. Even if somebody phones up to tell you your house is burning down, they ask first how you are."

You must identify the source of the note in case you have to go back to it for further details or if you need to refer to it in a reference note. There is no need to write all the publication details (author, title, publisher) on each note, if you develop a coding system to identify the source; simply use the key initial letters of the title. For example, *The Progress of Love* becomes POL. Code all sources the same way in your working bibliography. In addition to the source, you must also indicate the page reference for the information. Therefore, POL 3 indicates that the information is from page three of *The Progress of Love*.

If the quotation triggers an observation or an interpretation, you can make a brief comment below the quotation on the card. Such comments may be useful later. Here is an example:

POL 13

"There was a cloud, and poison, that had touched my mother's life. And when I grieved my mother, I became part of it."

(Notion of a secret not understood)

Although the focus in the essay is on "The Progress of Love," other stories by Alice Munro may contain relevant material. Again, since these are primary sources, you should use direct quotations.

Continue reading through the primary source or sources recording all ideas that are relevant to the question you have posed.

Secondary sources are handled in the same manner. Take one of your available sources, for example, *Alice Munro*, by E.D. Blodgett, and start looking specifically for information relevant to the question.

Information from secondary sources can be recorded as a direct quotation or in your own words. Generally speaking, it is a good idea to make a direct quotation if the information is concise even if you do not plan to quote directly from the source. This is a good idea because you may not have the source with you when you draft the essay, at which point you may wonder if your paraphrase or summary was accurate. Also, you may change your mind and want to use a direct quotation. On the other hand, there is no point in copying out paragraphs of text verbatim. If an author makes a valid point over two or three paragraphs, simply summarize the point in your own words.

In this instance, the point of interest made by E.D. Blodgett in *Alice Munro* on page seven is only one sentence long, so a verbatim quotation is in order:

AM 7

"Munro's manner of telling a story becomes a discovery procedure inviting the reader to attend upon how certain truths are reached."

In the following instance, the point made by E.D. Blodgett is somewhat longer and, consequently, it is summarized:

AM 145

POL deals with movement of time, coinciding the narrator's childhood with that of her mother's.

Continue reading through the relevant parts of book AM recording pertinent information. Do not make a card just because you find information that is vaguely "interesting." Ask yourself if the information will help answer the central question. Use the Table of Contents and Index in each book so that you can focus on the relevant pages.

Once you have completed book AM check it off on your working bibliography, and move on to the next available source—Helen Hoy's article, for example. Helen Hoy's article deals with the exposing of secrets in Munro's work. You decide to write down the sentence verbatim in case you wish to quote Ms. Hoy. Write it down accurately and use quotation marks to indicate that it is a quote and not a note. The source code (in this case UIM for "Alice Munro: Unforgettable Indigestible Messages") and page reference are recorded as usual.

UIM 5

" . . . Munro is rigorous in
exposing the conventions,
the self-deceptions . . . "

Carry on reading through source UIM recording information on your cards in the manner described.

You may have to alter your notemaking method slightly, depending upon the source. For instance, the following references come from the interview with Alice Munro by Kay Bonetti:

IKB

speaking of rural families:

"educating the sons was the
fathers' business and
educating the daughters
was the female business."

Note how the index cards record the context of the comments made by the author in the taped interview. Observe also how an ambiguous reference to "she" is made clear by the use of parentheses in the following quotation.

IKB

Munro speaking about POL:

"the great expanding thing she (mother)
had found was her religion & so
everything was subordinated to that,
including what would happen to her
daughter."

Continue working your way through all your available sources searching for information, ideas, and insights relevant to the question and systematically recording them on index cards.

- It is advisable to write just one piece of information on each card. That is why the smaller index card is recommended.

- If you do decide to write more than one note on a card ensure that they cover the same point.

- Your note cards have no special order so do not number them. They are all independent and each one is identified as to source.

- Do not use two cards for a lengthy note. Complete the note on the reverse side of the card.

- Do not confuse bibliography cards, which list sources, with research cards, which contain ideas and information.

- Use a file box or two-ring card folder to organize your cards.

- Each card should contain two items:

1. source code and page   2. note

Notepaper Method

Instead of using index cards for recording your responses and ideas, you can use notepaper. If you prefer using this method, you should still read pages 22 to 28 carefully because they contain many points about notemaking techniques that are not repeated in this section.

Rule a three-centimetre margin on the right side of the notepaper, but leave it blank. Work through your sources recording the relevant material in the centre column and identify the source and page reference in the left margin. Write on one side of the paper only. For an example of this technique, refer to the diagram below:

POL 3	"My father was so polite, even in the family. He took time off to ask me how I was. Country manners. Even if somebody phones up to tell you your house is burning down, they ask first how you are."	
POL 13	"There was a cloud, and poison, that had touched my mother's life. And when I grieved my mother, I became part of it." (Notion of a secret not understood)	
POL 14	"It seemed as if she knew something about me that was worse, far worse, than ordinary lies and meanness; it was a really sickening shame."	
POL 24	referring to commune which took over her parent's house: "They had displaced that life, hardly knowing it existed. They had set up in its place these beliefs and customs of their own which I hoped would fail them."	

Computer Method

You can do your research with a laptop computer, setting up computer files that are the equivalent of index cards or pages of notepaper. If you prefer using this method, you should still read pages 22 to 28 carefully because they contain many points about notemaking techniques that are not repeated in this section.

Modern word processing software is now so sophisticated that in most instances it is all that you need for recording ideas and information. The only thing that it may lack is a "data base" function that allows you to quickly sort your electronically stored index cards into various categories. You can buy computer software that will let you write, edit, retrieve, and sort cards on the screen. If you do buy such software, make sure that it is easy to use. Also, make sure that any text recorded using that software can be "exported" to the word processor with which you will ultimately write the essay.

No matter what type of software you use to record information and ideas, bear in mind that your notemaking should be just as detailed and comprehensive with regard to the identification and coding of sources as if you were using the other methods.

Whatever method you choose to record information and ideas, remember to keep these points in mind:

- A comprehensive system of notes is essential. It is exceedingly difficult to write an intelligent essay without good notes. Solid scholarship requires thought and hard work.

- Brainstorm continuously as you read and use your I.Q. Journal to list major ideas and insights.

- You are engaged in the pursuit of an answer to your question. Be rigorous in determining the relevance of your notes.

- Be fair and honest and do not select material to support a preconceived point of view.

- Build up a substantial collection of notes – the broader the base, the higher the pyramid.

- There is a time to stop digging and start shaping.[3] Learn to impose limits on your research.

WRITING THE ESSAY

INTRODUCTION

Now that the reading and recording stage has been completed, you can devote your efforts to the composition of your answer to the question. This is a crucial phase because the success of your essay hinges on your ability to communicate your argument or thesis clearly to the reader.

Clarity of argument is largely dependent upon style and structure. There are additional aspects: some practical, such as citation procedures; others philosophical, such as the subjectivity of selection. The subjectivity factor has to be dealt with as you construct and refine your argument. It is impossible for you to use all the material you encountered during the preparation. Therefore, you will have to select the significant and relevant material needed to answer your question. This selection process will be influenced by your individual perspective. Subjectivity (or frame of reference) may be defined as the manner in which people perceive, understand, and interpret the world according to their personal code of values. Bias (or prejudice) refers to a preconceived position based on the dogmatic selection of evidence.[4] Subjectivity is unavoidable. Bias is unethical.

Discipline and structure are requirements of successful expression, and form and order are essential elements in the creation of a readable essay. Contrary to what many people think, structure is a device to liberate creativity, not inhibit it.[5] The so-called ABC formula (Introduction, Body, Concluding Summary) is a simple and effective tool for promoting clear written communication. Only rarely would an essay benefit from a structure that deviates from this formula.

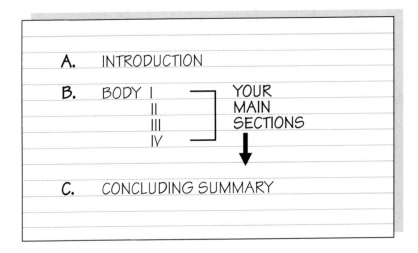

The following section on outlining emphasizes the importance of organization in developing clarity of argument before you start drafting your paper. Structure is a key component of clarity. Style, the other key component of clarity, is dealt with in section VI.

DEVELOPING OUTLINES

Once you have completed your reading and recording, you will have your notes organized on index cards, notepaper, or computer. It is difficult to write a final copy straight from these notes. A number of intermediate stages is necessary to ensure quality.

Remember that the purpose of your essay is to develop an answer or a response to your question and to articulate it in the form of an argument or thesis. The creation of an outline that imposes order on your notes is the first step in the process of organizing your material to achieve this purpose.

The following sections of this manual describe what might be called "conventional outlining." It is recognized that some students are used to alternative organizing systems such as "webbing," "mapping," and "tree diagramming." It does not matter what you call your organizing system; the important thing is to have one. As previously mentioned, it is a rare essay that does not benefit from some sort of structure and organization. But if an outline refuses to emerge from your notes, do not despair. Start getting words on paper anyway. In all probability, once you get going a structure of some sort will appear.

Basic Outline

During your reading and recording you may have already sketched out a tentative outline in your I.Q. Journal. Read through all your notes again, keeping your central question in mind. Try to isolate the main factors around which you can structure an answer. In the case of the Munro essay, we have isolated the three factors that appear to explain her broad appeal. You may remember that these factors started to become apparent during the preparatory reading stage. They can be itemized now in the Basic Outline as shown below:

```
BASIC OUTLINE

A.   INTRODUCTION

B.   I    FAMILY
     II   COMMUNITY
     III  RELIGION

C.   CONCLUDING SUMMARY
```

There is no magic number of sections in a Basic Outline — from three to six will handle most questions comfortably. After you have developed a Basic Outline, read through your note cards again and arrange them in groups according to the outline. If you used notepaper for recording your material, separate the individual notes with scissors and group them in the same way, in effect, making "cards" out of them.

It is a good idea to number the cards according to the section into which they fall. Use the upper right-hand corner of index cards or the empty right-hand column of the "cards" made from notepaper. For instance, all cards pertaining to "community" are labelled II, and all cards pertaining to "family" are labelled I.

```
TFTR 44                          II

"You see that judgement on
the faces of people looking
out of windows, sitting on
front steps in some little towns."
```

TMOJ 256   I

"How thoroughly we dealt with
our fathers and mothers . . .
how completely we filed them
away, defined them beyond
any possibility of change."

Some notes may have to be discarded as irrelevant if there is no place for them in either the major sections of the body of the essay or the introduction. Do not worry about discarding some cards; it would be a rare researcher indeed who did not end up with more notes than needed.

If you used a computer to record your material, you might find it easier at this stage to print copies of your notes and organize them manually. But if you do not feel this is necessary, then you can simply store all your "electronic notecards" in files named after the groups in your outline. If you used specific index card software, it is easy to group your notes in this manner. If you used a word processor and stored all your notes in one file, you might wish to use the "Word Search" feature of the word processor to accomplish the same end.

Skeleton Outline

Each section of the Basic Outline will have a substructure of its own. Hence, the next step is to read through your notes to determine the components of each section. Cards are efficient because you can isolate the sections and then spread the cards out on a table and search for the substructure. In our example we have gone through the classified notes and mapped out the substructure for each section on a page of notepaper. This stage is called the Skeleton Outline. Our example for the Munro essay follows:

SKELETON OUTLINE

A. INTRODUCTION *
1. Background
2. Issue
3. Question
4. Possible explanations
5. Thesis

B. I FAMILY
    1. Redefining one's parents
    2. Coming to terms with self-deception
    3. The limits of truth

    II COMMUNITY
    1. Censorious and judgemental
    2. Manners a mask
    3. Breaking the code

    III RELIGION
    1. Rural religion
    2. Puzzling out truth
    3. Failure to break free

C. CONCLUDING SUMMARY

---

*The contents of the Introduction are explained on pages 41–44.

Point-form Outline

Judgements and interpretations have to be developed and defended by sound reasoning and relevant material if your argument is to be credible and convincing. The use of the term "prove" is inappropriate in an essay because arguments, no matter how elaborate, seldom produce a "final answer." Most conclusions and interpretations in literary studies are tentative at best.

The Point-form Outline requires you to search through your notes and isolate the supporting detail for each section under the substructure of the Skeleton Outline. This should not be a lengthy process because you already have a good overall knowledge of the contents of your notes. However, it does require further selection. Do not attempt to cram all your notes into the essay for you will clutter it with debris and destroy the clarity of the answer. Be ruthless and reject the irrelevant notes.

Once again, avoid "stacking the deck" while selecting the material you plan to use. In longer essays you may have to address opposing viewpoints and ideas that run counter to your thesis. In such a case, conflicting arguments should be included at this stage so they can be challenged or countered later on.

Use as few words as possible in the Point-form Outline; do not rewrite your notes. You can always refer to your notes to check details when writing subsequent drafts.

There is rarely a need for a Concluding Summary in the initial drafting stages because new information is seldom included in the concluding section. However, if you have special points you wish to mention in the Concluding Summary, then add one to the Skeleton and Point-form Outlines.

Since the order of the main sections may change in the final copy, it is advisable to devote a separate page to each major section in the Point-form Outline. It is then very easy to rearrange the sections in the desired order when drafting the next stage. Notepaper is recommended for these early drafts or, alternatively, large index cards as there is insufficient room on the small index cards.

If you are using a computer, remember that most word processing programs have an "Outline" function built in. The outline function makes it easy for you to create outlines for it will automatically number the sections and subsections as you go along.

Developing the Skeleton and Point-form Outlines is not excessively time-consuming and the payoff lies in having a clear structure for paragraphing and weaving together the preliminary draft. It also enables you to determine if there are any weak spots in the argument. For instance, a Point-form Outline might show you that one of your main sections contains insufficient material to support your thesis and that it might be better to merge this with another section or eliminate it.

Here follows the Point-form Outline for the Introduction and the first major section of the Munro essay:

POINT-FORM OUTLINE

A.   INTRODUCTION
1. Background, including Issue
   - broad appeal of Munro
2. Question
   - why such varied readership
3. Possible explanations
   - style, exotic locale, content, technique
4. Thesis
   - puzzling out the truth
   - religion, community, family
   - universal relevance

B. I FAMILY
1. Intro paragraph
   - quote from TMOJ re: fathers and mothers
2. Redefining one's parents
   - difficult task
   - family secrets
   - different version of "truth"
3. Coming to terms with self-deception
   - restaurant incident
   - conflicting stories
   - self- deceptions
4. The limits of truth
   - failure of narrator to get ultimate answer
   - particular story with universal relevance

THE PRELIMINARY DRAFT

If you organize the sections of the Point-form Outline on separate pages, it is easy to rearrange them in ascending order of importance. Having worked extensively on the detailed outlines, you should have a clear idea of the relative importance of each section. Once you have rearranged the sections of the Point-form Outline, the shape of your paper will have emerged. It is time to start fleshing it out.*

How long should the essay be? This is one of the most common questions raised by students. In many cases the length of the paper will be determined by your instructor. If your instructor specifies a certain number of words, stay within ten percent of the specified figure. If no word limit is set, the length will be established by the demands of the question and your response to it. Shorter rather than longer is a sound rule to follow. Remember that your words should be weighed not counted.

With a detailed structure in place, it is a relatively easy task to start weaving the essay together. Having done the outlines, you should not be afflicted by "writer's block" at this point: you will know what you have to do. All the work that went into the outlines will now pay off.

If you are using a computer, you should take advantage of the fact that most modern word processing software allows you to work on two documents at the same time, either by means of two separate "screens" or by means of a split screen. Bring up your outline on one screen, and then begin writing the essay on the other screen. You can easily flip back and forth. You can also bring up the files that serve as your "electronic index cards" on one screen, and transfer

---

*There are a number of conventions of essay writing, such as quoting and documenting, that should be followed. These are discussed in sections IV and V, Quotations and Documentation. Consult these sections before proceeding with the preliminary draft since you will have to enter your citations in the draft. Because clarity of communication is so essential, you might wish to consult section VI on Style before writing the preliminary draft. Definitely consult it before writing the final draft.

relevant information from that screen onto the screen where you are writing the draft.

The "weaving" process whereby your Point-form Outline is turned into a readable essay requires that you express the ideas of the outline in structured paragraphs. The paragraphs are then "stitched" into the overall structure of the Skeleton Outline.

A paragraph is a series of sentences addressing one major idea or step in the development of your argument. If the idea addressed in a paragraph is substantial, the paragraph will be most effective if it follows the familiar ABC formula (Introduction, Body, Concluding Summary) with a topic sentence that states the main idea of the paragraph, followed by sentences that give supporting detail, and a concluding sentence that sums up the paragraph and clarifies its role in the development of your thesis.

If you have made a Skeleton Outline and a Point-form Outline, you will have no problem with paragraphing, for the Skeleton Outline isolates the paragraphs, and the Point-form Outline supplies the supporting detail for each paragraph. You must now make sure the sentences follow one another naturally and logically. This can be achieved by the careful use of transitional words such as furthermore, consequently, nevertheless, similarly, and likewise.

There also should be a smooth flow between paragraphs. This may require the use of short transitional paragraphs. There is no standard length for paragraphs. They can vary from several to ten or more sentences depending on function and significance.

There is no rigid prescription for paragraphing; if you see a good reason to deviate from the pattern arising from the outlines, by all means do so. But bear in mind that some organizing scheme is essential. Clarity of expression is a function of both style and structure with paragraphs providing the bridge between style and structure. Paragraphs with a central focus, explicit topic sentences, and suitable transitional words provide the unity, flow, and signposts that prevent the reader from getting lost in a maze of words.

Drafting the Introduction

The Introduction should prepare the reader by providing the background and purpose of the essay and by setting the general tone of your work. Although usually short, introductions are important because first impressions can influence the reader. Since English essays are scholarly studies, it is inappropriate to inject humour and sensationalism into the Introduction to catch the reader's attention.

The coffee filter diagram offers an effective framework for an Introduction for a major term paper or an extended essay using secondary sources. Short interpretive essays dealing with just the primary text might require an Introduction of only one or two paragraphs.

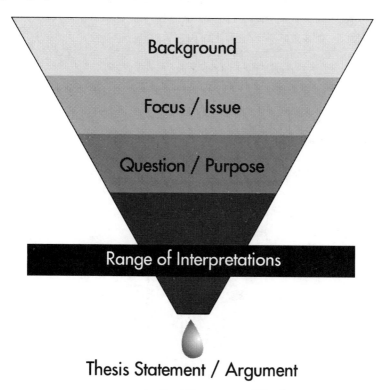

Background

Focus / Issue

Question / Purpose

Range of Interpretations

Thesis Statement / Argument

The coffee filter formula prepares the reader by first presenting the essential background information which will be largely descriptive, narrative, or biographical. The focus then shifts to the issue under investigation and its importance as a field of study. The reader must be made aware of the purpose of the essay and this can be indicated by stating the central question. If you find it difficult to integrate a question smoothly into the text of the Introduction, try stating the objective of the assignment in a more traditional way, such as "The purpose of this paper is to determine why Alice Munro's fiction has such broad appeal." However it is phrased, stating the purpose of the assignment is important because it provides the reader with a signpost showing the direction of the project.

The next step is to indicate the range of viewpoints and the nature of the intellectual debate surrounding your issue. If differing interpretations do not exist, as may be the case if your essay is a subjective appreciation of a primary text, then simply omit this section in the Introduction. In such an instance, the coffee filter changes its shape to that of a funnel.[6]

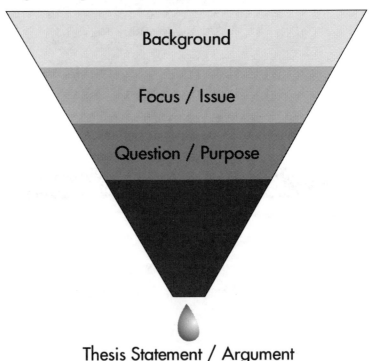

Background

Focus / Issue

Question / Purpose

Thesis Statement / Argument

Finally, state your thesis or argument (your answer to the question) clearly and concisely. It may be acceptable to use the first person in stating the thesis; for example, "I believe that Alice Munro's short stories have broad appeal because they deal with the search for truth hidden behind facades of social convention." Check with your instructor to ensure that the use of the first person is acceptable.

The paragraphing for an Introduction will not follow the same direct pattern as the main sections of the body, but will vary according to the content of the essay. Although there is a greater flexibility in structuring the paragraphs of the Introduction than those in the body, the coffee filter components of the Skeleton Outline still provide the basic organization.

Despite its brevity, the Introduction is an important and integral part of your essay. It will probably vary from about ten to twenty percent of the overall length of the essay but it must never overwhelm the body of your work. Some people prefer to write the Introduction first, others prefer to write it last. If you have followed the outlining and drafting procedures recommended in this manual, you will probably find it convenient to write the Introduction first.

Below you will find the Introduction to the Munro essay. This Introduction (in its final form after revision and editing) was crafted from the Point-form Outline on page 38. Note how it adheres quite closely to the basic introductory pattern described in the preceding paragraphs.

Alice Munro writes deceptively simple stories about presumably simple people—rural Ontario farm wives, small-town merchants, and retired married couples. Yet stories by this so-called "antiquarian miniaturist" (Fawcett 9) appear in such publications as *The New Yorker, Paris Review, Mademoiselle,* and *Gentlemen's Quarterly*—magazines designed for sophisticated urban readers.

The international interest in Munro's stories cannot be explained solely on the basis of the uniqueness of her style because it is as deceptively simple as the stories themselves. It cannot be explained on the basis of her exotic locales because rural Ontario is as ordinary as rural Nebraska. And it cannot be explained on the basis of sensational content because there is none: quite often virtually nothing "happens" in an Alice Munro story. What is the explanation?

Munro's impeccable technique, her "postmodern view of language"

(Perkin 5), is one reason for the international interest in her fiction; she is a master of compression, time-shifting, and subtle metaphor. But technique alone is not enough to explain a wide readership. Indeed, being a "writer's writer" is almost synonymous with not being widely read.

My reading of Alice Munro suggests that her ability to touch and move an international readership is based on the fact that much of her fiction deals with a search for the truth that is hidden behind facades of social convention and moral rectitude. This search is often hampered by the deceptions and white lies that are part of the fabric of family, community, and religious life. Although the Munro protagonist conducts this search in rural Ontario, it is a search with which all persons are familiar because they have had to puzzle out the secrets of their own family, community, and religion. The geographic and cultural landscape of Alice Munro's fiction may be particular, but the intellectual and emotional landscape is universal.

This introduction would be appropriate for an essay of moderate length. For shorter interpretive essays, you often need an introduction of only two paragraphs. For instance, if the essay focused exclusively on "The Progress of Love" and did not deal with secondary sources, the introduction might look like this:

Alice Munro writes deceptively simple stories about presumably simple people—rural Ontario farm wives, small-town merchants, and retired married couples. Yet her stories appear in magazines designed for sophisticated urban readers.

My reading of Alice Munro suggests that her ability to touch and move an international readership is based on the fact that stories such as "The Progress of Love" deal with a search for the truth that is hidden behind facades of social convention and moral rectitude. This search is often hampered by the deceptions and white lies that are part of the fabric of family, community, and religious life. Although the Munro protagonist conducts this search in rural Ontario, it is a search with which all persons are familiar because they have had to puzzle out the secrets of their own family, community, and religion. The geographic and cultural landscape of "The Progress of Love" may be particular, but the intellectual and emotional landscape is universal.

Drafting the Body

The body of the essay is the most important section and the longest. It is here that you use the relevant details from your notes to support your arguments and develop and substantiate your thesis.

A successful essay has the focus and clarity of a laser beam. Therefore, ensure that all supporting material is explicitly linked to the central theme and securely anchored in the argument. Avoid the tendency to pack the essay with irrelevant information because extraneous details will only serve to fragment the focus of the essay. Instructors and examiners look for incisive analysis and argument in an essay, not for chronological narrative, rambling description, or irrelevant biographical details. Your responsibility is to construct and advance a systematic, logical, and convincing thesis: one that is carefully structured, persuasively argued, substantiated with evidence, and clearly expressed.

The first major section of the Munro essay is reproduced below. It was crafted from the Point-form Outline on page 38. Like the Introduction, it appears in final form: it did not look this polished at the preliminary draft stage.

"The Progress of Love," the story that provides the title for Munro's sixth collection of short stories, illustrates the Munro process of "puzzling out" the truth behind facades. In "The Progress of Love" the middle-aged narrator Fame [short for Euphemia] sifts through her memories in an attempt to come to terms with the death of her mother and the meaning of her mother's life. Like many of Munro's stories, it is a story about the discovery and exposure of secrets (Blodgett 7). The discovery process is hampered by all three of the aforementioned barriers that hide or distort truth: family, community, and religion.

"How thoroughly we dealt with our fathers and mothers . . . how completely we filed them away, defined them beyond any possibility of change," says the narrator of another Munro short story, "The Moons of Jupiter" (256). Filed away in memory, "defined beyond any possibility of change," such parents continue to affect the values and belief systems of the Munro protagonist and hamper the search for truth.

Fame's puzzling out of the "truth" in "The Progress of Love" requires that she redefine her parents. This is a difficult task, for the secrets of families are often closely held. Each family member has a different version of a story, and each family member is subject to his or her own memory when recounting what happened—and the meaning of what happened—at a later date.

When Fame's Aunt Beryl takes Fame and her parents to a restaurant, Beryl casually tells Fame about an important incident that occurred many years ago when both Beryl and Marietta [Fame's mother] were young. It was an incident that was to affect Marietta deeply. Beryl's version of the event is substantially different than the version Fame has heard from her mother. Fame must ponder, and puzzles:

> Why shouldn't Beryl's version of the same event be different from my mother's? Beryl was strange in every way—everything about her was slanted, seen from a new angle. It was my mother's version that held, for a time . . . But Beryl's story didn't vanish; it stayed sealed-off for years, but it wasn't gone. (31)

As she ponders and puzzles, Fame muses on the difficulty of ferreting out the truth about "old marriages where love and grudges could be growing underground, so confused and stubborn . . ." (41). She learns she cannot trust her own memory about "all the things I know or have been told, about people I never even saw" (8). And she comes to terms with her own contribution to self-deception:

> How hard it is for me to believe that I made that up. It seems so much the truth it is the truth; it's what I believe about them [her parents]. I haven't stopped believing it. But I have stopped telling that story. (40)

Fame ultimately fails to find "the truth" about her family. But as the quoted passage reveals, she finds a truth she can live with. Any reader who has dealt with ambiguous events in his or her own family history knows that that is about all you can hope for. Fame's family is particular; indeed, an urban reader brought up in a foreign land might even find it peculiar. But there is nothing peculiar about the tangled webs of family myth and memory Munro describes. Munro's ability to trigger the reader's own memories about growing up and discovering family secrets is what gives her fiction a universal appeal.

Drafting the Concluding Summary

The final section is comprised of your conclusions that, after careful thought, form the most convincing answer to the question. In this section, you weave together the various threads of the thesis and sum up the major supporting points. It should not be a dull restating of the major sections but a subtle linking together of the main arguments. Sometimes it can be effective to start the concluding summary with the question since this reminds the reader of the purpose of the essay. But try to be more original than starting with a worn phrase such as "In conclusion." Avoid adding new information to support your thesis in the concluding summary since this will confuse the reader.

In addition to summing up the thesis, you might place your topic within a wider context or perhaps discuss aspects that need further investigation. You might also identify unresolved issues or show the broader significance of your work and suggest the implications for further research.

The concluding summary should be brief,* but it is important because it is the last opportunity to impress the reader with the validity of your arguments: remember that final impressions are usually lasting impressions. Below you will find the concluding summary of the Alice Munro essay. It is brief, it sums up the thesis, and it links it into a wider context. (The wider context is that all good fiction is more than just "story telling.")

Alice Munro's fiction, like all good fiction, is more than just the telling of a story. It touches the reader, creating little epiphanies of recognition. It does this because the search for meaning and truth beneath the deceptions and hypocrisy of family, community, and religious pieties is not something unique to Fame, the narrator of "The Progress of Love," nor is it unique to other Munro protagonists. All of us have, in one way or another, embarked upon a similar search.

---

*Short literary essays, especially if they deal exclusively with a primary text, might not necessarily require a concluding summary and, in some cases, instructors discourage concluding such an essay with a summary. When in doubt, ask your instructor.

THE FINAL COPY

Revising

If you want to produce a quality essay, you must revise and edit. There is no way around it. This means that you have to leave time for revising and editing. Revising involves rewriting sentences and restructuring paragraphs. Editing is the "fine tuning" that you do when revising is complete. If you do not start writing the first draft until the night before the deadline, then you do not have time for a second draft. You must make the time.

You may not wish to spend time on revising and polishing because of the extra work involved. But there is a close relationship between effort and quality, and a good piece of work will invariably reflect the extra care taken in its preparation. You will find revising and editing easier if you can set the essay aside for a few days before the final draft. Getting a little "distance" can sharpen your editorial eye to a remarkable degree.

It helps to approach revising with a positive attitude. By the time you reach the revising stage you have done a lot of hard thinking and a lot of hard writing. Admittedly, revising by hand or on a manual typewriter can be a tiring process, but the improved results will be well worth the effort.

The first step in the revising process is to read your draft aloud. (You can even tape it and play it back if you wish.) If it is difficult to read and sounds stilted, you are going to have to revise it until it flows naturally off your tongue. An essay that "speaks well" is invariably an essay that reads well. James Michener twice read aloud all 1238 pages of the manuscript of *The Covenant* before he was satisfied with it.

If it is inconvenient to read the essay aloud—because you might bother someone—then read the essay silently, moving your lips while you read. No cheating. You have to move your lips. If you do not, you will end up just skimming over the material you have written and the whole point of the exercise will be lost.

You should also give the essay to someone else to read. The other person will often pick up errors in logic or style of which you are unaware. You should also try reading your own work as if you were reading it for the first time.

Imagine that you have come across your essay in a magazine. Imagine that you know nothing about the subject of the essay. Take each sentence slowly, step by step. And as you do, ask yourself these questions:

- Can I understand what is being said?

- Does this sentence follow logically from the previous one?

- Do I have to know something that is not stated in this essay to understand it?

Work your way slowly through the essay and make notes whenever you encounter any kind of problem. Do not start skimming along admiring your handiwork and your clever wording. Concentrate. Read and interpret only what you actually wrote, not what you thought you wrote, or what you meant to write, or what someone should have known you meant to write. If you can turn yourself into an objective reader, you will become a good editor of your own work.

Apart from revising for continuity, clarity, and logical flow, you must also edit with the following considerations in mind:

- Pruning

  Most first drafts contain redundancies. Look for adverbs and adjectives that are not really necessary because the verb or noun they modify already says it all. Look for dragged-out expressions such as "at that point in time" that can be compressed. Make sure that every word is necessary and is doing some work. If it is not, get rid of it.[7] Brevity and precision are the key features of a pleasing style.

- Consistency

  Check to make sure you do not have singular subjects and plural verbs and vice versa. Check to make sure your use of pronouns is consistent. See section VI on Style for information on these matters.

- Qualifiers

  You may have used qualifying words such as "many," "some," and "always" in a casual way while writing the first draft. During re-writing you should check to make sure that qualifications are as precise as you can make them. Do not say "many" when the evidence indicates that there are only "several." Do not say "always" if you are not certain that is the case; say "frequently."

- Tone

  You may have had to struggle to write certain sections of the essay; other sections may have come easily. The sections that were tough to write may reflect this fact, while other sections may be quite breezy in tone. Level things out: lighten up the former and tone down the latter.

- Punctuation

  Proper punctuation can do much to improve the readability of your essay. If you did not pay attention to punctuation during the preliminary draft, pay attention to it while revising and editing. See Style, section VI, for tips on how to punctuate effectively.

Revising with a Word Processor

The word processor is a powerful editing tool. Many persons who use word processors tend to revise as they go—even at the first draft stage—because it is so easy. The tendency is to save the file back to itself so that the new improved version takes the place of the previous version on the disk. There is nothing wrong with this if you are making minor changes; in fact there is nothing wrong with this if you are making major changes and are convinced that you will never change your mind. If there is any doubt, keep renaming the file in a serial manner as your editing proceeds. For instance, if you originally named the draft "ESSAY," name the first revision "ESSAY1," and the second "ESSAY2," and continue in this manner. This gives you a safety valve if, as so often happens, you decide that the first or second version really was the best, or that it contains deleted material that, upon reflection, you would like to include. After you have produced the final document it is a simple matter to erase the intermediate files. Many instructors advise students to print a hard copy each time a major revision has been undertaken and label it with the appropriate file name. This protects you from losing track of interim drafts.

Do not get so caught up in the revision process that you end up reworking one or two sentences over and over in a search for the perfect opening paragraph. If that happens, leave well enough alone and get on with the job of completing the essay. You can come back to that paragraph later.

Although revising and editing are easy on a word processor, it is not easy to detect spelling or punctuation errors on a video monitor. Most persons find that they can detect errors more readily if they print a hard copy of the text. This is something you should bear in mind when doing your final polishing. Printing out an early draft has one other advantage: it shows you that the printer and printer ribbon are in working order and will be able to provide you with a final copy of your essay when you need it. The night before deadline is not the time to discover that although your essay is "in the computer" you cannot get it out.

If your word processor has a spelling checker, or grammar check program, make sure you take advantage of these options prior to printing the final draft. But remember that you must edit your work carefully even after you have used the software program because, although spell checkers are very sophisticated, they have no way of knowing that when you wrote "to" you meant to write "too" or "two."

Format

The appearance of your paper can be dramatically enhanced by using computer technology. Desktop publishing programs can ensure an attractive layout and laser printers with a variety of fonts can provide a clean, professional type. If you are using a dot matrix printer, make sure the type is easy to read. Most schools and universities have facilities accessible to students. Although giving an essay a professional appearance is desirable, remember that it is not finery but substance that is most important. All the same, instructors generally prefer a typed essay to a handwritten one.

Individual instructors sometimes have their own preferences with regard to format, so it is advisable to check manuscript requirements before starting the final copy. If your instructor has expressed no specific preference, format your essay in this manner:

- Use standard-sized white unlined paper and type on one side only.

- Leave at least a 2.5 cm margin all the way around the page and double-space the text.

- Number pages consecutively in arabic numerals in the upper right corner.

- Avoid section headings as they tend to disrupt the argument.

- A "ragged" right margin is recommended because the text is easier to read than justified right margins which can create uneven spacing.

- Do not staple the pages together if you are using endnotes, because instructors often like to remove the endnotes and refer to them as they read the essay.

- Always keep a backup copy of your essay. Keep your notes and drafts as well: they are your best defence against a charge of plagiarism.

The final packaging is important because the overall appearance of the essay can create a positive initial impact, thus making a good impression.

Title Page

The title page should be simple, clear, and neat. The following information is normally required on title pages for English essays:

1. Title: clear and concise but not normally in question form. Use a subtitle only if it helps to clarify the title.

2. Student name.

3. Course or class.

4. Instructor.

5. School/university/college.

6. Date.

Here is the title page of the Munro essay. This a common type of layout. Your instructor may ask for a different format.

The Appeal of Alice Munro

J.S. Henderson
English 101

Professor M. Snelgrove
Elbon College
February 1992

Table of Contents

A table of contents provides the reader with an outline of the structure of your essay. Most high school and undergraduate English essays do not require a table of contents. The example below shows the table of contents from a major research paper or extended essay. The letters of the alphabet correspond to the numbering used throughout the research and drafting stages. Do not refer to the term "body" in the table of contents. It is used in this guide merely to assist you in understanding the structure of an essay.

TABLE OF CONTENTS

A. INTRODUCTION
B.
    I . . . .
    II . . . .
    III . . . .
    IV . . . .
    V . . . .
C. CONCLUDING SUMMARY
D. APPENDIX
E. WORKS CONSULTED

Appendix

Depending on the nature of your essay, you may want to have an appendix. An appendix is a useful place to put essential information that is too extensive to be placed in the text or in a footnote. The material should be relevant to the theme of your paper and must be cross-referenced in either a footnote or in a parenthetical reference. An example of an appendix in an English essay would be a chronological listing of the works of a writer. Guard against the temptation to pack the appendix with unnecessary material. The Appendix is placed before the Endnotes and the Bibliography and each section is numbered and titled. See pages 103 to 114 of this manual for an example.

List of Sources

The format for listing sources is discussed in section V on Documentation. This is how the list of sources would be entered for the Munro essay:

WORKS CITED

Blodgett, E.D. *Alice Munro*. Boston: Twayne, 1988.

Fawcett, Brian. "Me and My Gang." *Books in Canada* Dec. 1991: 8–9.

Hoy, Helen. "Alice Munro: Unforgettable Indigestible Messages." *Journal of Canadian Studies* 26.1 (1991): 5-21.

Munro, Alice. Interview. By Kay Bonetti. Audiocassette. American Audio Prose Library, 1987.

Munro, Alice. *Dance of the Happy Shades*. Toronto: Ryerson, 1968.

—. *The Moons of Jupiter*. Markham: Penguin, 1983.

—. *The Progress of Love*. Toronto: McClelland and Stewart, 1986.

—. *Friend of My Youth*. Toronto: McClelland and Stewart, 1990.

Perkin, Russell. Letter. *Books in Canada* Mar. 1992: 5.

QUOTATIONS

Carefully selected quotations can illustrate and reinforce your arguments effectively. They can also lend an elegance to your writing. As a general rule, quote from primary material. However, excerpts from secondary sources can be used to provide credibility and additional authority for your arguments.

If you are challenging an opposing viewpoint in a secondary source, then quote the point of view before responding critically. While secondary excerpts may indicate the range and depth of your research, mere name-dropping of prominent authorities for effect should be avoided.

Remember that quotations by themselves do not constitute indisputable evidence. It is the strength of your arguments that will finally convince the reader of the validity of your thesis. Quotations must be firmly anchored in the text and explicitly linked to the thesis. They should not be parachuted into the essay as spacefillers. "To indulge yourself too often in the quoting of others' great thoughts is to run the risk of never learning to formulate your own."[8]

The proper citing of quotations is dealt with in the following section. In the examples of quotations that follow, citations have been omitted for purposes of simplicity.

Short, single-sentence quotations should be incorporated within the text of the essay and placed in double quotation marks. The quoted material should be woven into your writing and merged as naturally as possible within the text.

Example:

Munro's impeccable technique, her "postmodern view of language" is one reason for the international interest in her fiction.

Keep quotations brief, but if a longer quotation is necessary and if it consists of two or more sentences and comprises more than four lines, it should be separated from the text. The quoted passage starts on a new line ten spaces from the left margin and is usually introduced with a colon. Double-spacing is used and quotation marks are omitted.

Example:

Beryl's version of the event is substantially different than the version Fame has heard from her mother. Fame must ponder, and puzzles:

> Why shouldn't Beryl's version of the same event be different from my mother's? Beryl was strange in every way—everything about her was slanted, seen from a new angle. It was my mother's version that held, for a time . . . But Beryl's story didn't vanish; it stayed sealed-off for years, but it wasn't gone.

If it is necessary to omit part of a quotation, use three spaced periods (. . .) as shown in the previous example. This is known as an ellipsis. However, you must not alter the meaning of the passage or make it incomprehensible through your own omission of words.

If you have to insert words in a quotation to clarify its meaning, enclose them in square brackets.

Example:

> How hard it is for me to believe that I made that up. It seems so much the truth it is the truth; it's what I believe about them [her parents]. I haven't stopped believing it. But I have stopped telling that story.

If an error is present in the quoted material, use the Latin word *sic* (meaning "so" or "thus") to indicate it. Parentheses, square brackets, or underlining may be used for *sic*.

Example:

McGregor's Journal entry for the fifteenth of December contains the following cryptic comment on the relationship: "Lunched with Ian McTavish, he is still seathing [sic] about the delay."

It is important to distance yourself from quotations or ideas that are distinctly sexist. There are several ways you can avoid them. You can paraphrase the remark, replace the sexist words with bracketed substitutes, or use [sic] when appropriate.[9]

If you are quoting material between one and three lines long from a poem or a play, you may incorporate the excerpt in the text, enclosing it in quotation marks. Lines are separated by a slash.

Example:

In his final soliloquy, Hamlet expresses his determination to act with vigour and resolve: "O! from this time forth, / My thoughts be bloody, or be nothing worth!"

Quotations of more than three lines from poems or plays should be separated from the text and commence on a new line. Indent each line ten spaces from the left margin, omit quotation marks, and double-space the material.

Example:

In *The Prelude*, William Wordsworth emphasizes the restorative value of childhood experiences and memories:

> Such moments
> Are scattered everywhere, taking their date
> From our first childhood: I remember well,
> . . . .
> . . . . I am lost, but see
> In simple childhood something of the base
> On which thy greatness stands; . . .

Note that the row of ellipses here indicates the omission of a line or more of the poem.

Single quotation marks are used where a quotation occurs within quoted material.

Example:

"Williams said he had been subjected to `cruel and unusual punishment' during his confinement."

Generally, punctuation marks such as commas and periods are placed within the quotation marks, while colons, semicolons, question marks, and exclamation marks go outside the quotation marks. However, any punctuation mark that is part of the quoted material is included within the quotation marks.

Do not burden the text with excessively long quotations over seven or ten lines long; they should be placed in the appendix and referred to in a note or a parenthetical reference.

It is essential that you quote the material, including the punctuation, accurately. To alter the wording or meaning of a quotation or to use a quotation out of context is unethical.

Care must be exercised in quoting the writings and ideas of others so that you do not infringe copyright laws. There are methods for acknowledging and documenting your sources, thereby ensuring that you are not guilty of plagiarism. These reference procedures have been omitted from the quotation examples above to avoid confusion. They are explained in detail in the next section on Documentation.

Students are advised to consult one of the recommended manuals on the complexities and conventions of quoting. The examples used in this section are based largely on the procedures outlined in the latest edition of the Modern Language Association *Handbook*. So, too, are the quotations in the sample Munro essay, to which you might also wish to refer. Above all, be consistent in the method you use for quoting.

DOCUMENTATION

INTRODUCTION

I t is essential that you identify the sources you have used to develop and substantiate your arguments. It is especially important to document the evidence when you are making a controversial point. **Both direct quotations and paraphrased ideas must be acknowledged.** "Since you are a borrower at risk of being mistaken for a thief,"[10] failure to document sources constitutes plagiarism: a serious academic offence. Just as ignorance of the law is no excuse, there is no excuse for "accidental" plagiarism. However, factual information that is common knowledge need not be documented. For instance, you do not have to document a source for a statement indicating that William Shakespeare was born in Stratford-on-Avon.

Frequently, determining what is common knowledge is not easy, but your judgement will improve with practice. Document if in doubt is a safe rule to follow,[11] but do not overdo the use of references. It is a mistake to attempt to impress the reader with reams of footnotes or parenthetical citations. Common sense as well as ethics should govern your use of citations.[12]

Citing the authorities for information used in your paper gives credit to other writers for their ideas. It also enables the information to be checked for accuracy and guides the reader to additional sources of information on the topic.

Two major documentation or citation styles are used in the humanities: parenthetical in-text citations (the author/page method) and numbered footnotes/endnotes. Check with your instructor to find out which method to use. However, you should develop an understanding of each method, since they are both widely used. In this manual the in-text citations have been used in the Munro essay; the manual itself uses numbered endnotes.

There are no firm guidelines but, in general, parenthetical in-text citations are used in literature and linguistics papers and footnote/endnote references in papers in the other humanities. The basic elements of each are explained in the following pages under identical headings: Documenting Sources, Explanatory Notes, and Listing Sources. Sample citations are also provided. Because each section is self-contained, there is some necessary repetition.

AUTHOR/PAGE

Documenting Sources

The Modern Language Association (MLA) recommends identifying and acknowledging the sources of your information by providing the author's last name and page number in parenthetical references in the text. The reader can then refer to the list of sources at the end of the essay to obtain the bibliographic details.

Example:

Lincoln's death did not draw any "nobler expression" of national grief than Whitman's poem "O Captain! My Captain!" (Rossetti 143).

In the list of works at the end of the essay the reference would be entered as follows:

Rossetti, William Michael.   *Rosetti Papers*.   London: Sands and Company, 1903.

The in-text citation procedure enables the reader to determine the source quickly, but frequent parenthetical references tend to disrupt the reader's flow of thought. Try to reduce the number of your citations if possible. Improve readability by placing the citation at the end of a sentence or where a pause occurs and include the author's name in the text if possible.

Example:

As John Bailey, another Whitman biographer and critic said in 1926, "All true poets live in the universal" (180).

Some of the more common forms of parenthetical citations using the author/page system are shown below. For further details and more specialized forms you should consult chapter 5 of the *MLA Handbook*. Only the parenthetical reference is given in the examples below; the corresponding entry in the list of sources (Works Cited or Bibliography) is shown separately on pages 66–72.

Citing an entire work:

Charles Dickens' *Hard Times* is a novel of social realism.

Citing part of a work:

In *Timebends* Arthur Miller describes his confrontations with the House Un-American Activities Committee (328-35, 357-8).

Citing a multivolume work:

Strindberg's complex dramatic structure is perfectly expressive of another key expressionistic idea: the illusory quality of time and space (Gassner 2:780).

Citing a work listed by title:

The *Oxford Companion to English Literature* notes that W.H. Mallock is best known as the author of *The New Republic* (489).

Citing a work by a corporate author:

The *Canadian Women's Indexing Group* provides a retrospective index to 15 selected English- and French-Canadian feminist periodicals (130).

Citing works by the same author:

Turabian suggests using "ibid." when references to the same source follow consecutively (*Manual for Writers* 159).

Citing indirect sources:

His description of himself in 1882 as "a young man of a very revolutionary and contradictory temperament" (qtd. in Shaw and Weintraub 114) reveals the essence of his complex personality.

Citing literary works:

In his final soliloquy Hamlet expresses his determination to act with vigour and resolve: "O! from this time forth, / My thoughts be bloody, or be nothing worth!" (*Hamlet* 4.4.65-66).

In *The Prelude* William Wordsworth emphasizes the restorative value of childhood experiences and memories:

> Such moments
> Are scattered everywhere, taking their date
> From our first childhood: I remember well,
>
> . . . .
> . . . . I am lost, but see
> In simple childhood something of the base
> On which thy greatness stands; . . . (16–18, 68–70)

Citing two works:

In Thomas Hardy's novels there is a strong sense of the inevitability of character and environment in the working out of human destiny (Grimsditch 28; Abercrombie 40).

Citing multiple authors of a source:

Literary criticism has historically been a much more retrograde activity than the imaginative writing it studies (Stephens et al. 224).

Explanatory Notes

The MLA *Handbook* recommends that two types of notes be used with parenthetical citations. Content notes contain explanatory information. While this information might be relevant to the essay, it could detract from the development of your argument if inserted directly in the text. For example, a content note might explain that there is some question as to the precise publication date of the literary work that is the subject of the essay.

Bibliographic notes are used for critical comments on sources or for suggesting additional sources to consult. An example of a bibliographic note would be a note explaining that further information on the subject being discussed is available in other publications as well. Both content and bibliographic notes should be used sparingly.

When using these notes, place a superscript arabic numeral in the text and write the note after the corresponding number either at the bottom of the page as a footnote or on a separate page at the end of the paper as an endnote. Notes are numbered consecutively throughout the paper. When writing the note, indent five spaces and type the number in superscript followed by a space and then the note. If the note continues beyond one line, start subsequent lines at the left margin. It is customary to double-space endnotes and single-space footnotes and to leave a double space between individual notes. Examine the following examples.

Content Note

[1] To show the Duke's aggrandizing nature in his production of the play, the director, Jonathan Miller, made Isabella march off the stage when the Duke announced their marriage (McLuskie 95).

Bibliographic Note

[3] For other examples of verbal echoes of *Hamlet* in *Lord Jim*, see Part 2 of *Conrad and Shakespeare and Other Essays* by Adam Gillon.

Listing Sources

Brief in-text parenthetical references have to be linked to a master list of sources at the end of the essay. If you are listing just the sources cited in the text of your paper, you will probably use one of the following headings:

Works Cited, Sources Cited, Literature Cited, References Cited.

If, however, you included sources that proved useful in the preparation of the paper but were not all necessarily cited, you might use one of the following headings:

Bibliography, Select Bibliography, List of Sources, References, Works Consulted, Sources Consulted.

The more traditional term "Bibliography" actually means a list of books and is still widely used. However, because sources today range from books to interviews to computer programs, the *MLA Handbook* recommends using the term "Works Consulted."

The sources should be listed in alphabetical order by author on a separate page at the end of the essay. Do not number your source entries. If you have used index cards for your working bibliography, it is easy to arrange them in alphabetical order for compiling the final list of sources. A good word processing package makes it easy to format your bibliography. If your word processor does not have this feature, there are special software packages available for preparing bibliographies. It is unlikely, however, that you would need this software since you are not writing a major essay based on many sources.

A single list of sources should be adequate for most school and undergraduate essays. For longer research papers you may be required to classify your sources into primary and secondary material, or published and unpublished information. Note that the working bibliography recommended earlier in this guide suggested sources be grouped under headings such as "Books," "Periodicals," and "General." This was to encourage a diversity of sources. The final bibliography should not be classified in that manner.

If an annotated bibliography is required, you will have to make critical comments on the value of each source.

Example:

Livesay, Dorothy. *Right Hand, Left Hand.* Erin: Press Porcepic Ltd., 1977.
This is Livesay's account of her life in Paris, Toronto, Montreal, and Vancouver in the 1930s. It is most useful for an understanding of the political radicalization of her poetry.

Each bibliographic entry starts at the left margin. If it extends beyond one line, the second and subsequent lines are indented five spaces. Double-spacing is used throughout the list of sources. If there is no place of publication given, use N.p.; for no publisher, use n.p.; and if no date is provided, insert n.d.

Listed below are some of the more common forms of entering your sources. These are based on the latest procedures in the *MLA Handbook* and students are advised to consult chapter 4 for further details and more specialized forms.

Book:

One Author
Crichton, Michael. *Jurassic Park.* New York: Ballantine, 1990.

TWO AUTHORS
Howard, V.A. and J.H. Barton. *Thinking on Paper*. New York: Morrow, 1986.

MORE THAN THREE AUTHORS
Kaus, Carl H. et al. *Stages of Drama*. Glenview: Scott, 1981.

EDITOR/COMPILER
Howes, Barbara, ed. *Eye of the Heart: Short Stories from Latin America*. New York: Avon, 1973.

NO AUTHOR
Beowulf. Trans. David Wright. Harmondsworth: Penguin, 1960.

TRANSLATION
Tolstoy, Leo. *Anna Karenina*. Trans. David Magarshack. New York: Penguin, 1961.

CORPORATE AUTHOR
Aurora Art and Hugh Lauter Levin Associates. *Impressionism and Post-Impressionism*. New York: Park Lane, 1989.

MULTIVOLUME WORK
Durant, Will and Ariel. *The Story of Civilization*. 11 Vols. New York: Simon, 1965.

POEM IN AN ANTHOLOGY
Pound, Ezra. "The Seafarer." *A 20th Century Anthology*. Ed. W.E. Messenger and W.H. New. Scarborough: Prentice, 1984. 68-70.

PLAY
Shakespeare, William. *King Lear*. Ed. Alfred Harbage. New York: Penguin, 1986.

LATER EDITION
Strunk, William Jr. and E. B. White. *The Elements of Style*. 3rd ed. New York: Macmillan, 1979.

REPUBLISHED BOOK
Frost, Robert. *Poems*. 1916. New York: Washington Square Press, 1971.

OTHER LANGUAGE
Kosok, Heinz. *Geschichte der anglo-irischen Literatur*. Berlin: Erich Schmidt, 1990.

PAMPHLET

Johnston, Denis. *John Millington Synge*. Columbia Essays on Modern Writers 12. New York: Columbia UP, 1965.

Encyclopedia:

SIGNED ARTICLE

Young, Philip. "Hemingway, Ernest." *Encyclopedia Americana*. 1973 ed.

UNSIGNED ARTICLE

"Callwood, June." *Canadian Encyclopedia*. 1988 ed.

Newspaper:

SIGNED ARTICLE

von Lowenstern, Enno. "English Uber Alles." *New York Times* 9 Nov. 1990: A35.

UNSIGNED ARTICLE

"Earth Talks Sputter." *Globe and Mail* [Toronto] 4 Apr. 1992: A1.

EDITORIAL

"As the Waters Start to Rise." Editorial. *Daily Gleaner* [Fredericton, NB] 4 Apr. 1992: 6.

LETTER TO THE EDITOR

Mole, Dr. Kenneth. Letter. *The Times* 3 Nov. 1990: 13.

Journal:

CONTINUOUS PAGINATION

Marrouchi, M. Ben T. "Literature is Dead, Long Live Theory." *Queen's Quarterly* 98 (1991): 775-803.

SEPARATE PAGINATION

Breslin, Paul. "Two Cheers For The New Formalism." *Kenyon Review* ns 13.2 (1991): 143-148.

(*ns* indicates that it is a new series)

Magazine:

SIGNED ARTICLE

Matus, Irvin. "The Case for Shakespeare." *Atlantic* Oct. 1991: 64-72.

UNSIGNED ARTICLE

"Passion in Winnipeg." *Maclean's* 6 Apr. 1992: 45.

Dissertation:

UNPUBLISHED

Thornton, Patricia. "The Prison of Gender: Sexual Roles in Major American Novels of the 1920s." Diss. U of New Brunswick, 1976.

ABSTRACT

Linkskold, Jane M. "The Persephone Myth in D.H. Lawrence." *DAI* 49 (1989): 3733A. Fordham U.

Review:

BOOK

Towers, R. Rev. of *Friend of My Youth,* by Alice Munro. *New York Review of Books* 17 May 1990: 38-39.

FILM

Ansen, David. "How the West was Lost." Rev. of *Dances with Wolves,* dir. by Kevin Costner. *Newsweek* 19 Nov. 1990: 67-68.

PLAY

Ingram, Anne. "Production Proves Theatre Very Much Alive at U.N.B." Rev. of *Rosencrantz and Guildenstern are Dead* by Tom Stoppard. *Daily Gleaner* [Fredericton, NB] 6 Apr. 1992: 17.

Interview:

PERSONAL

McCormick, Edwin. Personal interview. 10 Jan. 1980, Toronto.

PUBLISHED

Gordimer, Nadine. Interview. "The Power of a Well-Told Tale." By P. Gray and B. Nelan. *Time* 14 Oct. 1991: 91-92.

RADIO/TELEVISION

Gordimer, Nadine. Interview. *Writers and Company*. By Eleanor Wachtel. CBC Stereo, Toronto. 26 May 1991.

RECORDED

Munro, Alice. Interview. By Kay Bonetti. Audiocassette. American Audio Prose Library, 1987.

Speech/Lecture:

Peck, M. Scott. "A New Psychology of Love, Traditional Values and Spiritual Growth." Lecture Series. The Centre of New Fire. Ottawa, 22 Sept. 1990.

Conference Proceedings:

Staines, David, ed. *The Callaghan Symposium*. Proc. of a Conference. 24-25 Apr. 1980. Ottawa: U of Ottawa P, 1981.

Film:

Garland, Patrick, dir. *A Doll's House*. With Claire Bloom and Anthony Hopkins. South Gate Entertainment, 1989.

Radio & Television Programs:

"Apartheid." Narr. Judy Woodruff. Prod. John Blake. *Frontline*. PBS. WBNE, Watertown. 10 May 1986.

Recording:

Shakespeare, William. *Twelfth Night*. Dir. Howard Sackler. Caedmon, SRS-M213, 1961.

Performance:

Hamlet. By William Shakespeare. Dir. John Wood. With Neil Munro and Edward Atienza. National Arts Centre, Ottawa. 9 Apr. 1979.

Work of Art:

Picasso, Pablo. *Still Life with Chair-Caning.* Musée Picasso, Paris.

Letter:

Frost, Robert. "Letter to Editor of the *Independent.*" 28 Mar. 1894. *Selected Letters of Robert Frost.* Ed. Lawrence Thompson. New York: Holt, 1964. 19.

Manuscript:

Hare, W.A. Diary, 1900. Hare Papers. National Archives, Ottawa.

All titles have been italicized in these examples. If you are using a word processor, titles may be boldface or italicized. If you produce your essay on a typewriter, then underline the titles.

When listing two or more books by the same author, enter the surname for the first entry only. For the next entry type three hyphens and a period, leave two spaces and enter the title and publication details. See the "Works Cited" for the Munro essay on page 55 for an example. Page 116 also serves as a model for preparing your list of sources.

The above procedures are from the *MLA Handbook.* Kate Turabian's *Manual for Writers* also explains the use of parenthetical in-text citations.

FOOTNOTES/ENDNOTES

Documenting Sources

Another method of acknowledging and identifying your sources is to use numbered notes. An arabic numeral is placed above the line at the end of the sentence or quotation and these reference numbers are numbered consecutively throughout the paper. The in-text numbers follow all punctuation marks except the dash. Each of these superscript reference numbers corresponds to an entry in either a footnote at the bottom of the page or to an endnote in a separate section at the end of the essay. Numbered documentation notes create less interruption in the reader's flow of thought than the parenthetical procedure.

Traditionally, footnotes have been used as documentation notes. However, it is becoming increasingly common to place all reference entries on a separate page at the end of the essay and to refer to them as Notes or Endnotes. In lengthy research papers and dissertations they can be placed at the end of each chapter. This practice has developed because it simplifies the typing process, reduces publishing costs, and is preferred by many readers. See page 115 of this manual for an example of reference endnotes.

The reference footnote has the advantage of easy access of information for the reader. This is especially true when reading dissertations on microform. Furthermore, recent word processing packages make it relatively easy to use the footnote format. Despite the forecasts, it certainly is not an outmoded method of documentation.

Footnotes are separated from the text by a solid line twenty spaces in length. Leave a blank line and beneath it indent the same number of spaces as your regular paragraph indentations. If you are using block paragraphs, then use either six, seven, or eight spaces for indenting your footnotes. Type the superscript number followed by the reference details without an intervening space. If the note continues on a second line, start at the left-hand margin and single-space the note. A double space is left between individual notes. When a work is mentioned in a reference note for the first time, the complete entry is given with the author's names in normal order. A shortened form is used for subsequent references (see page 79). If there is no place of publication given, use N.p.; for no publisher, use n.p.; and if no date is provided, insert n.d.

Endnotes are entered in a similar fashion on a separate page at the end of the essay. Title the page "Endnotes" or "Notes." You can use either superscript numbers (entered as explained above) or numbers typed on the line. In the latter case only, the number is followed by a period and two spaces before the reference details are entered.

Examples of the more common forms of reference notes are shown below; one of the recommended guides should be consulted for more specialized forms. The examples shown here are based largely on the procedures in the latest edition of *A Manual for Writers* by Kate Turabian, which is derived from the procedures recommended by *The Chicago Manual of Style*.

Book:

ONE AUTHOR
[1]Michael Crichton, *Jurassic Park* (New York: Ballantine, 1990), 61.

TWO AUTHORS
[2]V.A. Howard and J.H. Barton, *Thinking on Paper* (New York: Morrow, 1986), 18.

MORE THAN THREE AUTHORS
[3]Carl H. Kaus, et al., *Stages of Drama* (Glenview: Scott, 1981), 30.

EDITOR/COMPILER
[4]Barbara Howes, ed., *Eye of the Heart: Short Stories from Latin America* (New York: Avon, 1973), 40.

NO AUTHOR
[5]*Beowulf*, trans. David Wright (Harmondsworth: Penguin, 1960), 45.

TRANSLATION
[6]Leo Tolstoy, *Anna Karenina*, trans. David Magarshack (New York: Penguin, 1961), 30.

Corporate Author
[7]Aurora Art and Hugh Lauter Levin Associates, *Impressionism and Post-Impressionism* (New York: Park Lane, 1989), 50.

Multivolume Work
[8]Will and Ariel Durant, *The Story of Civilization*, vol. 10, *Rousseau and Revolution* (New York: Simon, 1965), 56.

Poem in an Anthology
[9]Ezra Pound, "The Seafarer," in *A 20th Century Anthology*, eds. W.E. Messenger and W.H. New (Scarborough: Prentice, 1984), 70.

Play
[10]William Shakespeare, *King Lear*, ed. Alfred Harbage (New York: Penguin, 1986), 3.4.41-45.

Later Edition
[11]William Strunk Jr. and E. B. White, *The Elements of Style*, 3rd ed. (New York: Macmillan, 1979), 20.

Republished Book
[12]Robert Frost, *Poems* (New York: Holt, 1916; reprint, New York: Washington Square Press, 1971), 44 (page reference is to reprint edition).

Other Language
[13]Heinz Kosok, *Geschichte der anglo-irischen Literatur* (Berlin: Erich Schmidt, 1990), 67.

Pamphlet
[14]Denis Johnston, *John Millington Synge*, Columbia Essays on Modern Writers, no. 12 (New York: Columbia UP, 1965), 14.

Encyclopedia:

Signed Article
[15]Philip Young, "Hemingway, Ernest," in *Encyclopedia Americana*, 1973 ed.

Unsigned Article
[16]"Callwood, June," in *Canadian Encyclopedia*, 1988 ed.

Newspaper:

SIGNED ARTICLE
[17]Enno von Lowenstern, "English Uber Alles," *New York Times*, 9 November 1990, A35.

UNSIGNED ARTICLE
[18]"Earth Talks Sputter," *Globe and Mail* [Toronto], 4 April 1992, A1.

EDITORIAL
[19]"As the Waters Start to Rise," editorial, *Daily Gleaner* [Fredericton, NB], 4 April 1992, 6.

LETTER TO THE EDITOR
[20]Dr. Kenneth Mole, letter, *The Times*, 3 November 1990, 13.

Journal:

CONTINUOUS PAGINATION
[21]M. Ben T.Marrouchi, "Literature is Dead, Long Live Theory," *Queen's Quarterly* 98 (Winter 1991): 775.

SEPARATE PAGINATION
[22]Paul Breslin, "Two Cheers For The New Formalism," *Kenyon Review*, ns 13, no. 2 (1991): 143.

(*ns* indicates that it is a new series)

Magazine:

SIGNED ARTICLE
[23]Irvin Matus, "The Case for Shakespeare," *Atlantic*, October 1991, 64.

UNSIGNED ARTICLE
[24]"Passion in Winnipeg," *Maclean's*, 6 April 1992, 45.

Dissertation:

UNPUBLISHED
[25]Patricia Thornton, "The Prison of Gender: Sexual Roles in Major American Novels of the 1920s" (Ph.D. diss., U of New Brunswick, 1976), 7.

ABSTRACT
[26]Jane M. Linkskold, "The Persephone Myth in D.H. Lawrence," *DAI* 49 (1989): 3733A (Fordham U), 69.

Review:

BOOK
[27]R. Towers, review of *Friend of My Youth,* by Alice Munro, in *New York Review of Books,* 17 May 1990, 39.

FILM
[28]David Ansen, "How the West was Lost," review of *Dances with Wolves,* directed by Kevin Costner, in *Newsweek,* 19 November 1990, 67.

PLAY
[29]Anne Ingram, "Production Proves Theatre Very Much Alive at U.N.B.," review of *Rosencrantz and Guildenstern are Dead,* by Tom Stoppard, in *Daily Gleaner* [Fredericton, NB], 6 April 1992, 17.

Interview:

PERSONAL
[30]Edwin McCormick, personal interview, 10 January 1980, Toronto.

PUBLISHED
[31]Nadine Gordimer, "The Power of a Well-Told Tale," interview by P. Gray and B. Nelan, *Time,* 14 October 1991, 92.

RADIO/TELEVISION
[32]Nadine Gordimer, interview by Eleanor Wachtel, "Writers and Company," CBC Stereo, Toronto, 26 May 1991.

RECORDED

[33]Alice Munro, interview by Kay Bonetti, American Audio Prose Library, 1987, audiocassette.

Speech/Lecture:

[34]M. Scott Peck, "A New Psychology of Love, Traditional Values and Spiritual Growth," Lecture Series, The Centre of New Fire, Ottawa, 22 September 1990.

Conference Proceedings:

[35]David Staines, ed., *The Callaghan Symposium: Proceedings of a Conference held in Ottawa 24-25 April 1980* (Ottawa: U of Ottawa P, 1981), 57.

Film:

[36]Patrick Garland, dir. *A Doll's House*, with Claire Bloom and Anthony Hopkins (London: South Gate Entertainment, 1989).

Radio & Television Programs:

[37]"Apartheid," narr. Judy Woodruff, prod. John Blake, *Frontline*, PBS, WBNE, Watertown, 10 May 1986.

Recording:

[38]William Shakespeare, *Twelfth Night*, directed by Howard Sackler, audiocassette SRS-M213, Caedmon, 1961.

Performance:

[39]William Shakespeare, *Hamlet*, National Arts Centre, Ottawa, 9 April 1979.

Work of Art:

[40]Pablo Picasso, *Still Life with Chair-Caning,* oil on canvas, 1912, Musée Picasso, Paris.

Letter:

[41]Robert Frost, "Letter to Editor of the *Independent,*" 28 March 1894, in *Selected Letters of Robert Frost,* ed. Lawrence Thompson (New York: Holt, 1964), 19.

Manuscript:

[42]W. A. Hare, "Diary, 1900," Hare Papers, National Archives, Ottawa.

Citing Indirect Sources:

[43]G.B. Shaw, "G.B. Shaw's Tribute to the Work of Henry George," *The Single Tax Review* IV (15 April 1905): 23, quoted in G.B. Shaw and Stanley Weintraub, *Shaw: An Autobiography: Selected from his Writings* (New York: Weybright and Talley, 1969), 114.

All titles have been italicized in these examples. If you are using a word processor, titles may be boldface or italicized. If you produce your essay on a typewriter, then underline the titles.

There is no need to give the complete entry for a subsequent reference to a source. If you have to refer to a work already cited in full, use an abbreviated format containing the author's surname and the page reference.

Example:

[6] Turabian 168.

If more than one of Turabian's books has been used you would have to include a shortened version of the title to identify it.

Example:

⁶ Turabian, *Student's Guide* 168.

If it is necessary to refer immediately to the same source, you may choose to use "ibid." which is the abbreviated form of the Latin word "ibidem" meaning "in the same place." For example, an immediate reference to the same page of Turabian's book would be cited:

⁷ Ibid.

If another citation to the same book by Turabian follows immediately, it would be entered in this way:

⁸ Ibid., 170.

It is not necessary to use ibid. Instead, simply repeat the author's name and give the new page number. Some instructors do not like the use of ibid. and other Latin abbreviations such as "op. cit.," and "passim" are becoming obsolete.

Explanatory Notes

There is another type of note that has a very different function than the documentary note. The explanatory note, sometimes called a supplementary or content note, is used for additional information. While this information might be relevant to the essay, it could detract from the development of your argument if inserted directly in the text. For example, it may be necessary to provide additional biographical information on an author. Cross references to other parts of the paper or to material in the appendix can also be made in this type of note.

It is more convenient for the reader to refer to explanatory information at the bottom of the page than to have to turn to the end of the essay. If you are using endnotes to document your sources, it is easy to distinguish the explanatory notes by using asterisks (*) or other symbols in the text to refer to the information in a footnote at the bottom of the page. For an example of an explanatory footnote see page 81 of this guide.

The "footnote" today tends to be of the explanatory type; the traditional reference footnote is usually placed at the end of the essay and is termed a "note" or an "endnote."

You should resist the temptation to place too much information in explanatory footnotes because this may distract the reader from the development of your argument in the text. If the information is relevant and necessary but extensive, place it in the appendix. Then use an asterisk in the text to refer the reader to the footnote which will refer to the material in the appendix.

Whatever method or combination of methods you use for explanatory material, it is important that you strive for consistency, simplicity, and clarity.

Listing Sources

A listing of all the information sources that proved useful in the preparation of the essay (not necessarily just those cited) should be appended to the essay.* Traditionally, this list has been called a **Bibliography** and it is probably still the most widely used term today. However, there are other designations that are frequently used. These include **Select Bibliography, Works Cited, Sources Consulted, Sources, References, List of References, Works Consulted,** and **Literature Cited.**

The sources should be listed in alphabetical order by author on a separate page at the end of the essay. Do not number the bibliographic entries. If you have used index cards for your working bibliography, it is easy to arrange them in alphabetical order to compile the final list of sources. Also, software packages are available that allow for quick preparation of bibliographies.

---

*Occasionally, you may quote an isolated idea from a work that has little relevance to the subject of your essay. For instance, you might quote a line from a song or a nursery rhyme. You should document the source in a footnote or endnote, but you do not necessarily have to enter it in your list of Works Consulted. For instance, you will see that three of the Endnotes in this book do not appear in the Works Consulted section.

A single list of sources should be adequate for most school and undergraduate essays. For longer research papers and dissertations you will be required to classify your bibliography into primary and secondary sources or published and unpublished material. Note that the classified structure of the working bibliography recommended earlier in this guide suggested that sources be grouped under headings such as "Books," "Periodicals," and "General." This was to ensure a diversity of sources and does not imply that the final bibliography should be classified in the same way.

If an annotated bibliography is required, you will have to make critical comments on the value of each source.

Example:

Livesay, Dorothy. *Right Hand, Left Hand.* Erin: Press Porcepic Ltd., 1977.
    This is Livesay's account of her life in Paris, Toronto, Montreal, and Vancouver in the 1930s. It is most useful for an understanding of the political radicalization of her poetry.

The format for bibliographic entries is similar to that used for documentation notes except for minor differences. One variation is the order of the names and another is the indentation of the entries. Each entry starts at the left margin with the author's surname listed first. If the entry extends beyond one line, the second and subsequent lines (which are single-spaced, not double-spaced) are indented five spaces. A single blank line is left between individual entries. If there is no place of publication given use N.p.; for no publisher, use n.p.; and if no date is provided, insert n.d.

Listed below are some of the more common forms of entering sources. They are based largely on the procedures described in Kate Turabian's *A Manual for Writers.* Students are advised to consult the manual for further details and more specialized forms.

Book:

ONE AUTHOR
Crichton, Michael. *Jurassic Park*. New York: Ballantine, 1990.

TWO AUTHORS
Howard, V.A. and J.H. Barton. *Thinking on Paper*. New York: Morrow, 1986.

MORE THAN THREE AUTHORS
Kaus, Carl H. et al. *Stages of Drama*. Glenview: Scott, 1981.

EDITOR/COMPILER
Howes, Barbara, ed. *Eye of the Heart: Short Stories from Latin America*. New York: Avon, 1973.

NO AUTHOR
Beowulf. Translated by David Wright. Harmondsworth: Penguin, 1960.

TRANSLATION
Tolstoy, Leo. *Anna Karenina*. Translated by David Magarshack. New York: Penguin, 1961.

CORPORATE AUTHOR
Aurora Art and Hugh Lauter Levin Associates. *Impressionism and Post-Impressionism*. New York: Park Lane, 1989.

MULTIVOLUME WORK
Durant, Will and Ariel. *The Story of Civilization*. Vol. 10, *Rousseau and Revolution*. New York: Simon, 1965.

POEM IN AN ANTHOLOGY
Pound, Ezra. "The Seafarer." *A 20th Century Anthology*. Edited by W.E. Messenger and W.H. New. Scarborough: Prentice, 1984. 68-70.

PLAY
Shakespeare, William. *King Lear*. Edited by Alfred Harbage. New York: Penguin, 1986.

LATER EDITION
Strunk, William Jr. and E. B. White. *The Elements of Style*, 3rd ed. New York: Macmillan, 1979.

REPUBLISHED BOOK
Frost, Robert. *Poems*. New York: Holt, 1916; reprint, New York: Washington Square Press, 1971.

OTHER LANGUAGE
Kosok, Heinz. *Geschichte der anglo-irischen Literatur*. Berlin: Erich Schmidt, 1990.

PAMPHLET
Johnston, Denis. *John Millington Synge*. Columbia Essays on Modern Writers, no. 12. New York: Columbia UP, 1965.

Encyclopedia:

SIGNED ARTICLE
Young, Philip. "Hemingway, Ernest." *Encyclopedia Americana*. 1973 ed.

UNSIGNED ARTICLE
"Callwood, June." *Canadian Encyclopedia.*. 1988 ed.

Newspaper:

SIGNED ARTICLE
von Lowenstern, Enno. "English Uber Alles." *New York Times*, 9 November 1990, A35.

UNSIGNED ARTICLE
"Earth Talks Sputter." *Globe and Mail* [Toronto], 4 April 1992, A1.

EDITORIAL
"As the Waters Start to Rise." Editorial. *Daily Gleaner* [Fredericton, NB], 4 April 1992, 6.

LETTER TO THE EDITOR
Mole, Dr. Kenneth. Letter. *The Times*, 3 November 1990, 13.

Journal:

CONTINUOUS PAGINATION
Marrouchi, M. Ben T. "Literature is Dead, Long Live Theory." *Queen's Quarterly*, 98 (1991): 775-803.

SEPARATE PAGINATION

Breslin, Paul. "Two Cheers For The New Formalism." *Kenyon Review*, ns. 13.2 (1991): 143-148.

(*ns* indicates that it is a new series)

Magazine:

SIGNED ARTICLE

Matus, Irvin. "The Case for Shakespeare." *Atlantic*, October 1991, 64-72.

UNSIGNED ARTICLE

"Passion in Winnipeg." *Maclean's*, 6 April 1992, 45.

Dissertation:

UNPUBLISHED

Thornton, Patricia. "The Prison of Gender: Sexual Roles in Major American Novels of the 1920s." Ph.D. diss., U of New Brunswick, 1976.

ABSTRACT

Linkskold, Jane M. "The Persephone Myth in D.H. Lawrence." *DAI* 49 (1989): 3733A. Fordham U.

Review:

BOOK

Towers, R. Review of *Friend of My Youth*, by Alice Munro. In *New York Review of Books*, 17 May 1990, 38-39.

FILM

Ansen, David. "How the West was Lost." Review of *Dances with Wolves*, directed by Kevin Costner. In *Newsweek*, 19 November 1990, 67-68.

PLAY

Ingram, Anne. "Production Proves Theatre Very Much Alive at U.N.B." Review of *Rosencrantz and Guildenstern are Dead*, by Tom Stoppard. In *Daily Gleaner* [Fredericton, NB], 6 April 1992, 17.

Interview:

PERSONAL

McCormick, Edwin. Personal interview. 10 January, 1980, Toronto.

PUBLISHED

Gordimer, Nadine. Interview. "The Power of a Well-Told Tale." By P. Gray and B. Nelan. In *Time*, 14 October 1991, 91-92.

RADIO/TELEVISION

Gordimer, Nadine. Interview by Eleanor Wachtel. "Writers and Company." CBC Stereo, Toronto, 26 May 1991.

RECORDED

Munro, Alice. Interview by Kay Bonetti. American Audio Prose Library, 1987. Audiocassette.

Speech/Lecture:

Peck, M. Scott. "A New Psychology of Love, Traditional Values and Spiritual Growth." Lecture Series. The Centre of New Fire. Ottawa, 22 September 1990.

Conference Proceedings:

Staines, David, ed. *The Callaghan Symposium: Proceedings of a Conference held in Ottawa 24-25 April 1980*. Ottawa: U of Ottawa P, 1981.

Film:

Garland, Patrick, dir. *A Doll's House*. With Claire Bloom and Anthony Hopkins. London: South Gate Entertainment, 1989.

Radio & Television Programs:

"Apartheid." Narr. Judy Woodruff. Prod. John Blake. *Frontline*. PBS. WBNE, Watertown. 10 May 1986.

Recording:

Shakespeare, William. *Twelfth Night*. Directed by Howard Sackler. Audiocassette SRS-M213. Caedmon, 1961.

Performance:

Shakespeare, William.   *Hamlet*.   National Arts Centre, Ottawa. 9 April 1979.

Work of Art:

Picasso, Pablo.   *Still Life with Chair-Caning*.   Oil on canvas.   1912. Musée Picasso, Paris.

Letter:

Frost, Robert. "Letter to Editor of the *Independent*." 28 March 1894. In *Selected Letters of Robert Frost*. Edited by Lawrence Thompson. New York: Holt, 1964. 19.

Manuscript:

Hare, W.A. "Diary, 1900." Hare Papers. National Archives, Ottawa.

Citing Indirect Sources:

Shaw, G.B. "G.B. Shaw's Tribute to the Work of Henry George." *The Single Tax Review* IV (15 April 1905): 23. Quoted in G.B. Shaw and Stanley Weintraub. *Shaw: An Autobiography: Selected from his Writings*, 114. New York: Weybright and Talley, 1969.

All titles have been italicized in these examples. If you are using a word processor, titles may be boldface or italicized. If you prepare your essay on a typewriter, then underline the titles.

When listing two or more books by the same author, enter the surname for the first entry only. For the next entry, type an eight-space line followed by a period; then enter the title and publication details.

> The above procedures are based largely on Kate Turabian's *A Manual for Writers*. The *MLA Handbook* also has a section on the use of documentation notes. The endnotes and bibliography of this manual have been entered according to MLA procedures.

STYLE

INTRODUCTION

The first prerequisite for becoming a competent stylist is to care about the craft of writing. Writing is a skill: sentences are built of words; paragraphs are assembled from sentences; essays or books are constructed out of paragraphs. Writing is also an art. However, it is worth noting that there is no literary equivalent to the genius of a Mozart, who amazed the crowned heads of Europe with his talent at the age of five. Great writers usually do not make their mark until their adult years. When their early attempts at writing are collected and published —often over their objections—the stories or essays frequently appear amateurish. The ability to write well is not something you are born with; writing is a craft you have to learn.

There are many guidebooks and manuals dealing with English usage. The titles of several of them appear at the end of this chapter. The section that follows deals briefly with various aspects of style as they relate to the writing of an essay. Read these sections prior to writing your preliminary draft. Also, you might wish to refer to the Appendix, which discusses ten common writing errors.

VOCABULARY

The judicious use of words is an important aspect of style. One carefully chosen word has much greater impact than a rambling phrase. A reputable dictionary and a thesaurus (or synonym finder) are essential companions for a writer.

TONE

An essay is a work of ideas, not moods or feelings. A style of expression that is appropriate for writing a short story is not appropriate for an essay. In an essay, your style should advance the argument, not get in the way of it. In other words, your style should not draw attention to itself.

Do not use contractions such as "wasn't," "hasn't," and "can't." They are a part of everyday speech, but they should not be used in an essay. Also, avoid slang and jargon. An essay is a serious piece of writing; therefore, the tone should be formal and scholarly but not dull and boring. As your writing skills improve, you will find your writing can be formal and scholarly and still be colourful and witty.

VERB TENSES

Most essays are written in the past tense, but literary essays are an exception to this general rule. If references are made to literary characters in an essay, they are referred to in the present tense even if they are from a past or future age, or even if the author who created them has been dead for years. There is a reason for this. Literary texts are not historical texts. Also, literary characters are not dead —they spring to life in the imagination of every reader who picks up the text. Consequently, Hamlet "is" ambivalent, not "was" ambivalent.

When you are referring to authors in relationship to their characters, use the present tense. Example: "Here Atwood is using satire to make the point that . . ."

Only use the past tense when you are making some type of historical reference. Example: "*The Apprenticeship of Duddy Kravitz* was Mordecai Richler's first commercially successful novel."

JARGON

Every academic discipline has its own jargon and code words. Some of these words are necessary and useful since they define a concept with great precision, but some of them are no more than big words designed to impress the reader. A beginning writer can find such words seductive, and there is nothing wrong with that; you would be a poor writer indeed if you did not want to constantly broaden your vocabulary. It is a mistake, however, to think that fancy or obscure words add to the quality of an essay. If you wish to use such words, make sure you know exactly what they mean and use them in the proper context. And do not overdo it. A good essay is not something written in a secret code that only the writer and the instructor can understand; a good essay should be accessible to any intelligent reader.

PERSONAL PRONOUNS

Do not weaken your arguments by the repeated use of the personal pronoun "I." "I think that," "I feel that," "It appears to me," and similar expressions serve no purpose since the reader knows it is you—not some committee—who is writing the essay and assumes the ideas in the essay are your own. If you do find it necessary to use "I," and your instructor does not object, use it: do not hide behind pretentious expressions such as "the writer" or "the author."

Avoid the use of the second person pronoun "you." It is often used in colloquial speech (if you go one block and turn left you will find the restaurant), and it is used in instructional manuals (it is used frequently in this book), but there is little place for "you" in academic writing. Do not write, "In the first act of *Romeo and Juliet* you find. . ." Try another construction, such as "The first act of *Romeo and Juliet* demonstrates that . . ."

Which pronouns, then, can be used? The first person plural "we" can be used effectively in places where your first instinct is to write "you," but do not use "we" to set up a phoney "buddy" relationship with the reader in the hope that he or she will accept everything you say without question. If you use such expressions as "thus we see," or "we see here that," make sure that what follows is something with which any reasonable reader would agree. If the conclusion that follows is arguable, do not use the pronoun "we." In this situation it is wiser to revert to the third person singular "one" and say, "thus one sees that . . ." This identifies you as the observer and interpreter, and courteously allows the reader to make up his or her own mind about the logic of your argument. However, use "one" sparingly. If it is used too often, your writing may appear pretentious. Also, do not use "one" to refer to writers other than yourself. For instance, do not say "although one could argue that . . ." and then quote a critic with whom you wish to take issue. Name the critic, and then take issue. If there is more than one critic, then say, "A number of critics have argued that . . ."

When in doubt about the acceptability of certain personal pronouns or expressions such as "the author of this paper," consult your instructor.

AVOIDING SEXIST EXPRESSIONS

"Man is the measure of all things," said the Greek philosopher Plato. This is an example of sexist language—language that tacitly assumes that only persons of the male sex can hold significant office or think significant thoughts. Times change, and language changes with the times. Sexist language that stereotypes people is no longer acceptable; it behooves the essay writer to recognize sexist expressions and replace them with acceptable nonsexist words or phrases.

In some cases a sexist slant can be avoided by simply substituting one word for another, such as "human" or "people" for "man," or "humanity" for "mankind." In other instances the substitution of a gender-neutral suffix ("chairperson" for "chairman") is sufficient. Sometimes it is more difficult to find a nonsexist substitute, but persevere; you will often be rewarded with a more precise word. If a substitution such as "fireperson" for "fireman" appears clumsy you can sometimes get around it by rewriting the sentence using a plural subject. For example, you can refer to "firefighters."

Pronouns present major problems because the English language does not have a gender-neutral personal pronoun that takes the place of "his or her." Some writers have adopted the practice of using "his/her" but this expression has not, as yet, been widely accepted and there are many readers of both sexes who find the term objectionable. That being the case, it is often better to avoid the problem by switching to a plural subject, as in the following example:

Each participant should bring his or her notebook.
Participants should bring their notebooks.

It is worth noting that the switch to a plural subject and a gender-neutral pronoun has resulted in a more concise sentence. There are some writers who, with the encouragement of some grammarians, have opted to use "their" as a singular pronoun.

Example:

Everyone should bring their notebook.

Eventually this kind of construction may be widely accepted. At present it is not, and there are many readers who will assume that the writer thinks that "everyone" is plural instead of recognizing a purposeful attempt to avoid a sexist expression. Therefore, if you want to use "their" as a singular pronoun, check with your instructor first.

There are resources available to help you in your search for nonsexist expressions. See the list of recommended books at the end of this section.

PUNCTUATION

Most writers, with good reason, are more concerned with words than with punctuation. However, paying careful attention to punctuation can pay dividends: it can improve the appearance and readability of your essay to a remarkable degree.

Think of punctuation marks as nothing more than little time delays. That was their original purpose. They were devised to facilitate the public reading of prose or poetry by marking off the pauses. When reading became more of a private activity than a public one, the emphasis of punctuation switched to clarifying the text to avoid ambiguity. But a writer should keep the original purpose of punctuation in mind. Prose that captures the rhythms of human speech is seductive. Good essayists know this.

The Period

If we arbitrarily give the comma a time-delay value of one, then dashes and semicolons have a value of two, colons three, and periods four. Since periods control sentence length, they have a profound effect upon the overall pace of your prose. A good fiction writer will vary pace to invoke mood or to convey emotion, but pace is just as important in nonfiction as fiction; in fact, it can be more so. Be on guard against very long sentences filled with commas. You run the risk of losing your reader. Break them up into smaller sentences.

When editing, bear in mind that a procession of sentences of equal length induces boredom. Seek out those sentences that are related by way of subject and try replacing the periods between them with semicolons if you feel you want to slow the pace a bit, or with "and" if you do not. In the process of creating some longer sentences you will inadvertently create some shorter sentences as well. A mix of short and long sentences produces a pleasing rhythm, and the statements you make in the shorter sentences will seem more emphatic.

The Comma

Commas control the pace of a sentence just as periods control the pace of a paragraph. The trick with commas is to use just the right number of them. If you use too many, your sentences become jerky. If you use them too sparingly, your sentences tend to produce confusion and incomprehension. How to strike a happy medium? The simplest way is to just write naturally and let the commas fall where they may. Then go back to the beginning and either read aloud or silently while moving your lips. As you proceed, eliminate those commas that get in the way of an orderly flow and maintain only those commas that are essential for clarity of meaning or are instrumental in maintaining the pace you desire.

The Semicolon

Many writers avoid the semicolon either because they are afraid they might use it incorrectly or because they consider it a little too "fancy." However, the semicolon is one of the most useful punctuation marks in the wordsmith's toolbox. The semicolon has a time-delay value approximately halfway between the time-delay values of the comma and the period. It comes in handy for separating two short sentences which could stand independently with a period between them, but which are closely connected in sense. Example: "People do not only read because they seek information; they also read for pleasure."

Remember that you cannot combine such short sentences with commas; that is known as a "comma splice" error.

Semicolons are also useful for cleaning up a long comma-strewn sentence. Look for those commas that separate the major sub-sections of the sentence and replace them with semicolons; this can improve the readability of a long sentence to a remarkable degree.

If you plan ahead, you can use semicolons to string together many independent clauses, thus purposely creating one of the aforementioned sentences. Such sentence structures can be useful when you are concluding an argument; the conclusion seems more inevitable if it is arrived at in this manner. Also, the writing appears more elegant than if you had switched to a numerical or alphabetical point-form format. But remember: If you are going to use this technique, do it well. Do not sacrifice clarity for elegance.

The Colon

Generally, the colon is used to introduce lists or quotations; many writers shy away from using it in other circumstances. But it can be useful since its time-delay value is slightly longer than that of the semicolon, hence it serves very nicely when you want to isolate a word or phrase. Example: "Macbeth schemes to get the one thing that is apparently most important to him: power." This kind of punctuation can be very effective as long as you do not overdo it. Try experimenting with the colon by putting it in where you want to grab the reader's attention.

Parentheses

Parentheses (or curved brackets) serve to create footnotes in the body of a sentence. These references, explanations, or "by the way" remarks are not essential to the sentence and the sentence should read just as well without the parenthetical expression (what you put between the brackets) as with it. Extremely long parenthetical expressions serve only to distract the reader and should be avoided.

Not too long ago, curved parenthetical brackets were the only brackets available to a writer using a typewriter. Computers and electronic typewriters now allow the writer to use other types of brackets—the kinds one encounters in books that have been professionally typeset.

Square brackets are used to set off a clarifying remark of your own within a quotation. Example: "Harold returned from the war [Vietnam War] depressed and exhausted."

Square brackets are also used to enclose *sic* (Latin for "thus") when you want to indicate an error in the original.

The Dash

The time delay of a single dash is more or less equivalent to that of a semicolon, while that of a pair of dashes is more or less equivalent to that of a pair of commas. Whether used singly or in pairs, the dash tends to pack more psychological punch than the other stops. Dashes should be used sparingly; this is especially true for academic writing.

Single dashes are useful when you want to tack an afterthought onto a sentence—like so. Pairs of dashes are used to give parenthetical remarks a little more punch. Example: Margaret Atwood's *Survival*—a controversial attempt to apply thematic criticism to Canadian literature—was published in the 1970s but it is still being discussed today.

There is no way of reproducing on a typewriter the long dash known as an "em dash" (—) used in typeset books. But you can create a typewritten equivalent of the em dash by striking the hyphen key twice in succession. Example: Margaret Atwood's *Survival* -- a controversial attempt to apply thematic criticism to Canadian literature published during the "Canlit" ferment of the early 1970s -- is still being discussed today.

Double-hyphen dashes are recommended for a relatively long parenthetical remark (like the one in the above example) because they make it stand out clearly. Computer users often have the capability of producing the wider range of dashes available to typesetters.

The Exclamation Mark

If you are not writing dialogue, there is little need for exclamation marks, even in informal writing. Exclamation marks have no place in an essay, which is a formal work. If you feel you need an exclamation mark to pound home your point, then quite likely you are not making good use of the other punctuation marks at your disposal. Experiment with the sentence structure. You should be able to get the effect you want by other means.

RECOMMENDED BOOKS

The Practical Stylist by Sheridan Baker

A Short Guide to Writing About Literature by Sylvan Barnet

A Dictionary of Modern English Usage by H.W. Fowler

The Complete Plain Words by Sir Ernest Gowers

The Nonsexist Word Finder: A Dictionary of Gender-Free Usage by Rosalie Maggio

The Canadian Writer's Handbook by William E. Messenger and Jan de Bruyn

The Handbook of Nonsexist Writing by Casey Miller and Kate Swift

On Writing Well by William Zinsser

Publication details for these titles can be found in the bibliography at the back of this book.

CONCLUDING SUMMARY

E very essay is, to some extent, an exploratory trip into unknown intellectual territory. This manual has not provided you with a detailed "map" for your trip. No manual could do that, for its writer has no way of anticipating the territory you choose to explore. But this manual does provide you with a list of "provisions" for your trip, a sense of the direction you should take, and a little cautionary advice that will help prevent you from exploring paths that will not ultimately lead to your goal.

A well-equipped hiker who knows about the rules of survival in the woods is more likely to overcome adversities and reach his or her goal than is a tourist wandering aimlessly without even a compass to give a sense of direction. Likewise, you are far more likely to produce a successful essay if you have a method that allows you to get the best out of your material.

This manual gives you a method. If you write your essay according to the process described in the preceding pages, you will never find yourself "lost in the woods." That is not to say that you will not run into difficulties, but when you do, you will be able to look upon them as challenges to be overcome, not invitations to panic.

As you commence your exploration, bear in mind that your personal responses and insights are more likely to create an interesting or provocative essay than a dry recitation of what others have had to say about the text. And, as you approach your goal, remember that although clarity of argument is crucial, a literary essay — like a figure-skating performance — is assessed not only on "technical merit" but also on "artistic impression." Therefore, try to finish with style and grace.

APPENDIX

BIBLIOGRAPHIC AIDS

Articles in scholarly journals and popular magazines are an excellent source of information because they are usually concise, specific, and current. Periodical indexes and abstracts are essential tools because they enable you to locate articles relevant to your subject in thousands of magazines and journals. The following are just a few of the many indexes that are useful for humanities research:

> *Abstracts of English Studies*
> *American Humanities Index*
> *British Humanities Index*
> *Essay and General Literature Index*
> *Film Literature Index*
> *Play Index*
> *Short Story Index*
> *Studies on Women Abstracts*

The basic difference between Abstracts and Indexes is that the former not only index the articles but also summarize the subject matter. Abstracts usually scan journals containing more advanced research. You might wish to start with the indexes and then move on to the abstracts.

Citation Indexes stand in a class of their own. Even though they can be used for a subject search, they really enable the researcher to identify related writings by indicating sources in which a known work by a given author has been cited. The *Arts and Humanities Citation Index* lists items from over 6000 of the world's leading journals and is published three times a year, the third issue being the annual compilation. Although Citation Indexes are more complex to use than abstracts and regular indexes, most libraries display an explanatory chart showing a sample search.

Periodical indexes can be either very specific, such as the *Play Index*, or very general, such as *Reader's Guide to Periodical Literature*. When searching through the indexes and abstracts, it is advisable to peruse them systematically and sequentially year by year to avoid missing a volume. Some indexes start at the beginning of the century, while others are very new. It is even possible to delve into journals and magazines in the nineteenth century by using *Poole's Index to Periodical Literature* or *Wellesley's Index to Victorian Periodicals*. The needs of your assignment will determine whether you should use early or current periodicals.

Thousands of magazines and journals are published around the world each year. Some journals are devoted entirely to individual authors and their works such as *The Faulkner Journal* and *James Joyce Quarterly*. It is possible for you to determine which particular publications cover your subject area by consulting one of the following directories:

> *Canadian Serials Directory*
> *Irregular Serials and Annuals*
> *The Serials Directory*
> *The Standard Periodical Directory*
> *Ulrich's International Periodicals Directory*
> *Willing's Press Guide*

These directories include more than just periodicals:* they also list magazines, newsletters, government publications, yearbooks, and newspapers. The publications are classified by subject and complete bibliographic details are usually provided, including

---

*Periodicals comprise popular magazines and scholarly journals, whereas Serials cover periodicals as well as newspapers, conference proceedings, reports, yearbooks, and newsletters.

where they are indexed. Some of these directories also provide a list of abstracts and indexes.

A number of publications provide annual reviews of developments in their disciplines or commentaries on publications published during the year. These include:

American Literary Scholarship

Film Review Annual

The Year's Work in English Studies

Additional review publications may be located in the serials and periodicals directories listed on the previous page.

Bibliographies are publications listing books, articles, and other sources on specific topics and they can be accessed through most on-line catalogues. They are especially useful because someone else has done the searching for you. Once published, however, they can become dated. On the other hand, many bibliographies are published annually. The following are just a few of the more useful bibliographies:

Annual Bibliography of English Language and Literature

Bibliographia Canadiana

Bibliography: Women and Language

Cambridge Bibliography of English Literature

International Bibliography of the Theatre

MLA International Bibliography

A Shakespeare Bibliography

The Bibliographic Index is published three times a year, the third issue being the annual compilation. It is a subject list of bibliographies published separately or appearing as part of books or articles, and it is the most comprehensive guide to specific source material.

Masters theses and doctoral dissertations are useful for both content as well as source information in their bibliographies. Consult indexes such as the following for university theses and dissertations on topics that you are researching:

American Doctoral Dissertations

Canadian Theses

Comprehensive Dissertation Index

Dissertation Abstracts International

> *Index to Theses with Abstracts*
> *Masters Abstracts International*
> *Theses in English Literature*
> *Theses on English Canadian Literature*

Biographical indexes are indispensable if you are studying an individual:

> *American Women Writers*
> *Biography and Genealogy Master Index*
> *Biography Index*
> *Contemporary Authors*
> *Directory of American Scholars*
> *The New York Times Obituary Index*
> *The Annual Obituary*

Book reviews may enable you to determine the reliability of a book, and they will often provide additional information and insights on your subject:

> *An Index to Book Reviews in the Humanities*
> *Book Review Digest*
> *Book Review Index*
> *Canadian Book Review Annual*

Most periodical and newspaper indexes have sections on book reviews either under "Book Reviews," "Reviews," or in a separate section.

Many speeches, lectures, and presentations are delivered each year at conferences and conventions. Transcripts are often made available and they are accessible through indexes such as the following:

> *Bibliographic Guide to Conference Publications*
> *Directory of Published Proceedings*
> *Index to Social Science and Humanities Proceedings*
> *Proceedings in Print*

Newspapers are a valuable source of information. Like periodicals, there are indexes that will give you quick access to newspaper articles and editorials. The following list is a sample of many newspaper indexes:

Canadian News Index
The New York Times Index
Index to the Times
The Wall Street Journal Index

The application of computer technology to the news industry has resulted in many newspapers developing on-line indexes such as the *New York Times* in *Nooz* and the *Globe and Mail's InfoGlobe*. There are publications that provide lists of newspapers and indexes:

Checklist of Indexes to Canadian Newspapers
Gale Directory of Publications and Broadcast Media

There is a time lag between publication date and catalogue date for books. If you wish to discover the latest books on your subject, consult the *Cumulative Book Index*. It is a worldwide bibliography of books, classified by subject and published monthly with bound annual cumulations.

Should you wish to identify books available commercially on your topic but not held in your library, then consult references such as:

American Book Publishing Record
Books in Print
Canadian Books in Print
Forthcoming Books
International Books in Print
Whitaker's Books in Print

Obviously, your library will not house all existing publications but, fortunately, an inter-library loan system allows you to borrow material from other libraries. Most libraries have access to one of the following computerized networks which will indicate the sources of particular titles:

CRL (Center for Research Libraries)
DOBIS (Dortmunder Bibliothekssystem)
OCLC (Online Computer Library Center)
RLIN (Research Libraries Information Network)
UTLAS (University of Toronto Library Automation System)
WLN (Washington Library Network)

Another reference for establishing repositories of sources is the massive *National Union Catalog* and its supplements. If you wish to locate a journal not held in your library, consult the *Union List of Serials* and the *New Serial Titles*. Canadian researchers should consult the *Union List of Serials in Social Sciences and Humanities in Canadian Libraries*. Should you wish to determine which libraries hold special collections of sources on your subject, then refer to *Subject Collections*. Other guides include *Directory of Special Libraries* and *Information Centres and Research Collections in Canadian Libraries*. If you require a source from another library, discuss the inter-library loan procedure with a reference librarian.

Computer technology is transforming libraries and searching procedures. Mention has already been made of various computerized networks for inter-library loans and of the on-line catalogue that is rapidly replacing the card catalogue. These systems must not be confused, however, with external data base searching which is often referred to as On-line Reference.

It is now possible to search data bases around the world with ease and speed as major vendors such as *Dialog*, *BRS* (Bibliographic Retrieval Service), and *SDC* (System Development Corporation) provide instant access to hundreds of data bases from which you can retrieve print-outs of sources on your research topic. Most libraries offer computer searching of external data bases, but there are costs attached to this service to cover communication and royalty fees. Fortunately, vendors usually offer discount rates in the evening.

Many vendors have also put their data bases on compact discs, known as CD-ROM, and these can be searched in the library, usually at no cost. The CD-ROM version of a data base is not as current as the on-line system, but it is nevertheless very useful and relatively easy to consult. There are hundreds of data bases now available on CD-ROM, such as the following:

ERIC (Education)

FRANCIS (Arts and Social Sciences)

Humanities Index

MLA (MLA Bibliography)

The reference librarian will be able to indicate which data base is the most appropriate for your topic. You should investigate the process of data base searching because it is becoming an increasingly useful skill in research and writing.*

Although it may seem old-fashioned in the age of computer technology, browsing can be a very effective means of expanding your list of sources. You can locate your "browsing area" in the library by using the catalogue to determine which stacks hold books on your subject. By running your eye along the shelves you will often discover useful sources. And by checking tables of contents and indexes you will often pinpoint pertinent information in sources that would not be revealed in a catalogue search. A careful scrutiny of bibliographies and references in books on related topics to yours will often turn up additional sources. The reference shelves can be an especially profitable area for browsing.

In addition to the many reference sources already mentioned, you will find that the reference shelves contain a wide assortment of other material:

> Encyclopedias, e.g., *Cambridge Encyclopedia of Language*
>
> Handbooks, e.g., *A Handbook to English Literature*
>
> Research Guides, e.g., *Literary Research Guide*
>
> Dictionaries, e.g., *Dictionary of Literary Biography*

There are published guides, classified by subject areas, that will assist you in determining the availability of reference material on your topic:

> *Guide to Reference Books*
>
> *Walford's Guide to Reference Material*
>
> *Guide to Reference Sources*

These guides also list periodical indexes. All reference works in your library will be accessible through the main catalogue, but remember that reference material may not be removed from the library.

---

*For a discussion of the advantages and disadvantages of data base searching, see pages 85–93 of Thomas Mann's excellent manual, *A Guide to Library Research Methods*, published by Oxford University Press.

This manual lists only English language titles because of space limitations. There are numerous works in other languages in each of the categories mentioned. If you do not read other languages, you still can gain access to other cultures and perspectives by reading works in translation. The *Index translationum* and *Canadian Translations/Traductions Canadiennes* index translated books, while the *Translations Register-Index* lists unpublished translations into English.

Much information is stored in microform today because of space limitations in libraries. Microfiche and microfilm are the two most common microforms. Material in microform includes out-of-print books, newspapers, periodicals, dissertations, pamphlets, indexes, and catalogues. There are a number of guides to this material such as the following:

> *An Index to Microform Collections*
>
> *Microform Research Collections*
>
> *National Register of Microform Masters*
>
> *Subject Guide to Microforms in Print*

Microform holdings are frequently listed in the main catalogue. Knowing how to work with microfilm and microfiche readers is an essential asset in research and writing today.

There is a wide range of nonprint material available in the form of photographs, interviews, films, and television and radio programs. The following are just a few of numerous catalogues for films and television programs:

> *Britannica Films and Video*
>
> *National Film Board of Canada Film and Video Catalogue*
>
> *PBS Video*
>
> *Penguin Video Source Book*
>
> *Shakespeare on Screen*

The *Media Review Digest* is an annual guide to reviews of nonprint media.

Many libraries have special audio-visual rooms with catalogues and equipment. Holdings may include films, slides, filmstrips, records, compact discs, laser discs, and video- and audio-cassettes. Some libraries even permit overnight loans.

The current interest in oral history has resulted in libraries and archives developing collections of audio-taped material. Refer to guides such as *Oral History Collections* and *Oral History: A Reference Guide and Annotated Bibliography* to determine the accessibility of oral material pertinent to your project. *On Cassette* is an extensive bibliography of material on audio-cassette. Consider interviewing and taping experts in your field or approaching eyewitnesses such as observers at a literary event. Professors and teachers with special interests can also provide useful bibliographic leads.

COMMON WRITING ERRORS

Most instructors likely have their own list of the top ten stylistic errors. Here follows one such list:

1. The confusion of "its" and "it's."

Heartbreak House has been praised for the subtlety of it's art, the depth of it's poetic feeling, and the fascination of it's symbolism.

"Its" is a possessive pronoun. "It's" is a contraction of the sentence "it is." It is easy to confuse these two words because an apostrophe is commonly associated with a possessive, as in "Mary's," or "John's." But, in this case, "its" is the gender-neutral equivalent of "his" or "hers" and, like those two possessives, there is no apostrophe.

2. The confusion of "whose" and "who's."

Among others who experienced heartbreak was the Nurse who's husband left her and turned to burglary.

"Whose" is a relative pronoun. "Who's" is a contraction of "Who is." Thus, you say "Who's at the door?" meaning "Who is at the door?" and "Whose coat is this?" when you want to know the owner of the coat.

3. The use of "like" as a conjunction rather than a preposition.

Joseph listens like a good student should.

"Like" can be used as a preposition before a noun or pronoun. Examples: He runs like the wind. You should try to be like him. It is an error to use "like" in place of "as" before a subordinate clause which has its own verb. For example, "He is unhappy, like we all are" should be "He is unhappy, as we all are." Furthermore, "like" cannot replace "as" if a verb is absent but implied, as in the case in the example above, where it is clear that Joseph should listen *as* a good student should *listen*.

4.   Incorrect verb form.

But I don't think I could have went to see the film in a theatre.

"Could have went" for "could have gone" and "lie" for "lay" are the usual errors in verb forms. "Lie" and "lay" are especially troublesome. Remember: People lie, things lay. Thus you would say, "John was lying on the couch and his book lay beside him."

5.   Lack of agreement between subject and verb.

Faulkner, through the use of simple yet powerful images, create a motion picture on paper.

The error here was to use a plural verb to go with the plural word that immediately precedes it. The true subject of the sentence is "Faulkner," which requires the singular verb "creates."

6.   Lack of agreement between pronoun and antecedent.

For Gabriel, the snow represents his wife's individuality; like each and every snowflake each person is different with their own lives.

Words such as "everyone," "someone," and "each" are singular and require a singular verb. Consequently it should be "life," not "lives." (Since each is singular, it also takes a singular possessive pronoun; it should be "his," "her," or "his or her," not the plural possessive pronoun "their.")

7.   Lack of clear reference.

Coffins and ravens were discussed at the supper table which are rather obvious expressions of death.

The vague and imprecise use of "which" leads to vague and imprecise sentences. This rearrangement of the sentence structure is just one of many that would clear up the ambiguity: "Coffins and ravens—rather obvious expressions of death—were discussed at the supper table."

8. Unnecessary switching of tense.

The other is an orderly who is solitary, timid, physically fit ,and handsome. As the story began a sense of jealousy arose between the officer and the orderly.
The first sentence is in the present tense, the second switches to the past tense. Remember: English literature papers usually demand the present tense at all times.

9. Sentence fragments.

The description of the blanket showing that he feels sick and too old for the love he has for Anna.
This is not a sentence because there is no verb, just a participle. Substitute "shows" for "showing" and you have a sentence, albeit not a very good one.

10. The use of "is when" and "is because."

A good example of meanness is when Midge and Ronnie are arrested.
"Is when" and "is because" are sloppy colloquial expressions. Verbs such as "is" and "was" are verbs of being and should not be followed by subordinate clauses. Use "occurs when" instead.

There are, of course, many more grammatical and syntactical traps than the ten listed here. To avoid stumbling into them, consult one of the grammar texts listed at the end of section VI on Style. Reading such books is not as tedious as it might appear. One thing you will discover as you peruse such books, is that there are very few arbitrary rules of English usage. Most rules exist to make meaning precise and unequivocal.

ENDNOTES

[1] Kate L. Turabian, *Student's Guide for Writing College Papers*, 3rd ed. (Chicago: U of Chicago P, 1976) 31.

[2] Turabian, 26-30.

[3] Alden Todd, *Finding Facts Fast* (Berkeley: Ten Speed, 1979) 10.

[4] R.J. Shafer, ed., *A Guide to Historical Method* (Homewood, Illinois: Dorsey, 1974) 101.

[5] Edward de Bono, *Cort 1, Teacher's Notes* (New York: Pergamon, 1973) 7.

[6] Sheridan Baker, *The Practical Stylist* (New York: Harper, 1990) 43.

[7] William Zinsser, *On Writing Well*, 4th ed. (New York: Harper, 1990) 7.

[8] Gordon Taylor, *The Student's Writing Guide for the Arts and Social Sciences* (Melbourne: Cambridge UP, 1989) 160.

[9] Rosalie Maggio, *The Nonsexist Word Finder: A Dictionary of Gender-Free Usage* (Boston: Beacon, 1988) 170.

[10] David B. Pirie, *How To Write Critical Essays* (London: Methuen, 1985) 91.

[11] Sylvan Barnet, *A Short Guide to Writing about Literature*, 6th ed. (New York: HarperCollins, 1992) 231.

[12] Joseph Gibaldi and Walter S. Achtert, *MLA Handbook for Writers of Research Papers*, 3rd ed. (New York: MLA, 1988) 155.

WORKS CONSULTED

Baker, Sheridan. *The Practical Stylist*. 7th ed. New York: Harper, 1990.

Barnet, Sylvan. *A Short Guide to Writing about Literature*. 6th ed. New York: HarperCollins, 1992.

Clanchy, John and Brigid Ballard. *How to Write Essays: A Practical Guide for Students*. Melbourne: Longman, 1981.

Fowler, H.W. *A Dictionary of Modern English Usage*. Oxford: Clarendon, 1968.

Gibaldi, Joseph and William S. Achtert. *MLA Handbook for Writers of Research Papers*. 3rd ed. New York: MLA, 1988.

Gowers, Sir Ernest. *The Complete Plain Words*. 3rd ed. London: HMSO, 1986.

Maggio, Rosalie. *The Nonsexist Word Finder: A Dictionary of Gender-Free Usage*. Boston: Beacon, 1988.

Mann, Thomas. *A Guide to Library Research Methods*. New York: Oxford UP, 1986.

Messenger, William E. and Jan de Bruyn. *The Canadian Writer's Handbook*. 2nd ed. Scarborough, Ontario: Prentice-Hall, 1986.

Miller, Casey and Kate Swift. *The Handbook of Nonsexist Writing*. 2nd ed. New York: Harper, 1988.

Pirie, David B. *How to Write Critical Essays*. London: Methuen, 1985.

Shaw, Harry. *McGraw-Hill Handbook of English*. 4th ed. Toronto: McGraw-Hill Ryerson, 1986.

Stewart, Kay L. et al. *Essay Writing for Canadian Students*. 2nd ed. Scarborough, Ontario: Prentice-Hall, 1985.

Strunk, William Jr. and E.B. White. *The Elements of Style*. 3rd ed. New York: Macmillan, 1979.

Taylor, Gordon. *The Student's Writing Guide for the Arts and Social Sciences*. Melbourne: Cambridge UP, 1989.

Turabian, Kate L. *A Manual for Writers of Term Papers, Theses, and Dissertations*. 5th ed. Chicago: U of Chicago P, 1987.

—. *Student's Guide for Writing College Papers*. 3rd ed. U of Chicago P, 1976.

Watson, George. *Writing A Thesis*. London: Longman, 1987.

Zinsser, William. *On Writing Well*. 4th ed. New York: Harper, 1990.